Abbé Wai

Beekeeping For All

Simple and Productive Beekeeping

Northern Bee Books

Translated from the original French version of *L'Apiculture Pour Tous* (12th edition) by Patricia andDavid Heaf.

© Patricia Heaf and David Heaf, July 2007

First print edition. Taken from the 5th electronic English edition with corrections.

Published by Northern Bee Books
Scout Bottom Farm
Mytholmroyd
Hebden Bridge HX7 5JS (UK)

Important note on legislation:
This translation was made from the 1948 French edition.
Whilst some beekeeping practices may not have changed since then, it is possible that legislation has changed, for example that mentioned on pages 67 and 68.
Readers are therefore advised to check the current statutes and bylaws that are in force in their locality.

Printed by Lightning Source, UK

ISBN 978 - 1 - 904846 - 52 - 9

Cover Design: D&P Design and Print

Abbé Warré

Beekeeping For All

Simple and Productive
Beekeeping

Ainsi le voyageur qui, dans son court passage,
Se repose un moment l'abri du vallon,
Sur l'arbre hospitalier, dont il goûta l'ombrage,
Avant que de partir, aime graver son nom.

So the traveller who, in his short journey,
Rests a while in the shelter of the vale
On the hospitable tree, whose shade he enjoys,
Before leaving, likes to carve his name.

Lamartine

Before leaving, I would like, dear bees, to carve my name on these leaves, blessed shrub that has taken all its sap from around your dwelling place.
In its shade, I have rested from my weariness, have healed my wounds. Its horizon satisfies my desires for there I can see the heavens.
Its solitude is more gentle than deep. Your friends are visiting it. You enliven it with your singing.
And because you do not die, dear bees, you will sing again and for ever, in the surrounding foliage, where my spirit will rest.
Thank you.

E. Warré

Contents

The purpose of beekeeping

Apiculture or beekeeping is the art of managing bees with the intention of getting the maximum return from this work with the minimum of expenditure.

Bees produce swarms, queens, wax and honey.

The production of swarms and queens should be left to specialists.

The production of wax has some value, but this value is diminished by the cost of rendering.

The production of honey is the main purpose of beekeeping, one that the beekeeper pursues before everything else, because this product is valuable and because it can be weighed and priced.

Honey is an excellent food, a good remedy, the best of all sweeteners. We shall go into this in more detail. And we can sell honey in many forms just as we can consume it in many forms: as it is, in confectionery, in cakes and biscuits, in healthy and pleasant drinks – mead, apple-less cider, grape-less wines.

It is also worth noting that beekeeping is a fascinating activity and consequently rests both mind and body.

Furthermore, beekeeping is a moral activity, as far as it keeps one away from cafés and low places and puts before the beekeeper an example of work, order and devotion to the common cause.

Moreover, beekeeping is a pre-eminently healthy and beneficial activity, because it is most often done in the fresh air, in fine, sunny weather. For sunshine is the enemy of illness just as it is the master of vitality and vigour. Dr Paul Carton wrote: 'What is needed is to educate a generation in disliking alcohol, in despising meat, in distrusting sugar, in the joy and the great benefit of movement'.

For the human being is a composite being. The body needs exercise without which it atrophies. The mind needs exercising too, otherwise it deteriorates. Intellectuals deteriorate physically. Manual workers, behind their machines, suffer intellectual deterioration.

Working on the land is best suited to the needs of human beings. There, both mind and body play their part.

But society needs its thinkers, its office workers and its machine operatives. Clearly these people cannot run farms at the same time. But in their leisure time (they must have some of it) they can be gardeners and beekeepers and at the same time satisfy their human needs.

This work is better than all modern sports with their excesses, their promiscuity, their nudity.

Thus if the French were to return to the land they would be more robust, more intelligent. And as the wise Engerand said, France would again become the land of balance where there would be neither the agitations, nor the collective follies that are so harmful to people; it would become again a land of restraint and clarity, of reason and wisdom, a country where it is good to live.

And let us not forget the advice of Edmond About: 'The only eternal, everlasting and inexhaustible capital is the earth'.

Finally, one more important thing: the bees fertilise the flowers of the fruit trees. Apiculture thus contributes greatly to filling our fruit baskets. This reason alone should suffice to urge all those who have the smallest corner of orchard to take up beekeeping.

According to Darwin, self-fertilisation of flowers is not the general rule. Cross-fertilisation, which takes place most commonly, is necessitated because of the separation of sexes in flowers or even on different plants; or because of the non-coincidence of maturity of pollen and stigma or by the different morphological arrangements which prevent self-fertilisation in a flower. It happens very often that if an outside agent does not intervene, our plants do not fruit or they yield far less; many experiments demonstrate this.

As Hommell put it so well: the bee, attracted by the nectar secreted at the base of the petals, penetrates to the bottom of the floral envelope to drink the juices produced by the nectaries, and covers itself with the fertilising dust that the stamens let fall. Having exhausted the first flower, a second presents a new crop to the tireless worker; the pollen it is carrying falls on the stigma and the fertilisation which, without it, would be left at the mercy of the winds, takes place in a way that is guaranteed. Thus the bee, following its course without relaxation, visits thousands of corollae, and deserves the poetic name that Michelet gave it: the winged priest at the marriage of the flowers.

Hommell even attempted to put a figure on the benefit that resulted from the presence of bees. A colony, he said, which has only 10,000 foragers should be considered as reaching barely average, and a large stock housed in a big hive often has 80,000. Suppose 10,000 foragers go out four times a day, then in 100 days this will make four million sorties. And if each bee before returning home enters only twenty-five flowers, the bees of this hive will have visited 100 million flowers in the course of one year. It is no exaggeration to suppose that on ten of these flowers, at least one is fertilised by the action of the foragers and that the resulting gain would be only 1 centime for every 1,000 fertilisations. Yet in spite of these minimal estimates, it is evident that there is a benefit of 100 francs a year produced by the presence of just one hive. This mathematical conclusion is irrefutable.

Certain fruit producers, above all viticulturists, set themselves up in opposition to bees because bees come and drink the sweet juices of fruit and grapes. But if we investigate the bee closely we soon notice that they ignore the intact fruits and only empty those with pellicles that are already perforated by birds or by the strong mandibles of wasps. The bee only gathers juice which, without it, would dry up and be wasted. It is totally impossible for bees to commit the theft they are accused of, because the masticatory parts of its mouth are not strong enough to enable it to perforate the fruit pellicle that protects the pulp.

The benefits of beekeeping

I pity those who keep bees only to earn money. They deprive themselves of a very sweet enjoyment.

However, money is necessary to live. Money is useful to those who like to spread happiness around themselves.

Consequently it is justifiable to imagine that this could result from beekeeping.

But reading certain books and certain periodicals may lead to error on this point.

The lies

To encourage a return to the land or to deceive those who return there, beekeeper committees or some anti-French people published some staggering things in the newspapers. Perhaps there were also selfish beekeepers among them professing poor results so as not to create competition.

Thus a prominent beekeeper claims that a harvest of only 10 kg is a rare maximum. At the other extreme, a professor asserts that honey harvests should average 100 kg per hive if rational beekeeping methods are adopted.

A doctor declares that in America a single hive can yield an average annual harvest of 190 kg of honey, and that it is up to us to make it as much. Doubtless this would be by giving each hive 200 kg of sugar. But would not the fraud be exposed?

The truth

No type of hive, no method of beekeeping turns stones into honey. Neither do they make the beekeeper any wiser, or increase queen fertility or improve the ambient temperature. As a result the yield of a hive varies from one region to another, from one hive to another and from one year to another, just as does the nectar wealth of the region, queen fertility, temperature and the skill of the beekeeper.

When I lived in the Somme, I had an average annual harvest of 25 kg per hive. In a region with a high nectar yield one can harvest more. Here at Saint-Symphorien, in a region which is poor for nectar, I average only 15 kg. To be exact: in 1940 I had hives that cost me 300 francs each. Each gave me a harvest of 15 kg. Now the price of honey was fixed at 18 francs wholesale, 22 francs retail. Furthermore, each hive required one and a half hours of my time in the course of the year.

One can see with this how work and capital are rewarded in beekeeping, even in a region poorer in nectar.

Beekeeping is a good school

Coppée said that good fortune is giving it to others. Good fortune accrues to the souls of the elite. Now good fortune is not always possible, but you can find a considerable fortune in nature.

With flowers it is the beauty that endlessly rejuvenates itself. With dogs it is the boundless faithfulness, even in misfortune – unfailing recognition. The bee is a mistress and a delightful teacher. She provides an example of a wise and reasoned lifestyle, which gives solace from life's annoyances.

The bee contents herself with the nourishment provided in the surroundings of the hive, without adding anything to it and without taking anything away from it. No ready-made meals; no imported early fruit or vegetables.

The bee, however well provided she is, does not consume more than is absolutely necessary. No gluttony.

The bee makes use of her terrible sting and dies in doing so in order to defend her family and her provisions. Otherwise, even when she is foraging, she gives way peacefully to people and to animals. without recrimination, without a fight. She is a pacifist, but not weak.

Each bee has its task according to its age and abilities. It fulfils its task without desire, rebellion or anger. For the bee there is no humiliating work.

The queen lays tirelessly, thus assuring the perpetuation of the stock. The workers lovingly share their activity between the tender larvae, the hopes of the colony's future, and the fragrant fields where the honey is harvested from dawn to dusk. No place in a buzzing colony for the useless. No parliaments; for this quiet populace has neither a taste for new laws nor the leisure for futile discussion.

We call the laying bee the queen. This is incorrect. There is neither king nor queen nor dictator in the hive. Nobody is in charge, yet all work in the common interest. No egoism.

The bee observes the law that is as healthy as it is imperative, a law often overlooked by humans: 'you earn your bread by the sweat of your brow'. And I observe that the sweat of the bee, just in cleansing her body, is useful to her in another way. Her sweat, in changing into scales of wax, provides the bee with the materials that she uses to make her wonderful cells, a clean storehouse for her provisions, a soft cradle for her young. It is so true that the observance of natural laws is always rewarded.

Bees work day and night without respite. They only take a rest when there is no work to do. Not even a rest at the weekends. In the home of the bees there are neither pensioners nor retirees.

And here is the song of the bees that Théodore Botrel sang:

I said one day to the bee
Rest a little now,
Your striving to be like
This pretty blue butterfly
On the rose or the pansy,
See, it swoons in day-dreaming
Yes... but, me, I'm in a hurry,
Said the bee to me, in passing.
Showing her the dragonfly,
I said to her, another day
Come, from dawn to dusk,
Dance like her, when it's your turn
Don't you admire it, subtle,
Waltzing over there on the lake?
Yes... but me, I am useful
Said the bee to me, leaving.
Yesterday, before the door
Of its little temple of gold
I caught sight of it, half dead,
Heavy with its pollen again
Rest yourself, poor creature
I said to her while helping her
Yes... when my task is done,
The bee said to me as she died.

Henry Bordeaux said "What I admire most in the bee colony is the bee's total disregard for itself; she gives her self wholly to a job she will not enjoy – joy in the effort and giving of herself".

And for me bees are what birds were for André Theuret:

"When I hear the bees buzzing in the foliage, I dream with the slight feeling that they are singing in the same way as those I used to hear in my childhood, in my parents' garden".

One good thing about bees is they always seem to be the same. Some years pass; we age, we see our friends disappear, revolutionary changes take their effect, illusions fall one after the other, and yet, amongst the flowers, the bees that we have known from childhood modulate the same musical phrases, with the same freshness of voice. Time seems not to have taken its toll on them, and, as they hide themselves to die, as we never help them in their agony, we can imagine that we always have before our eyes those that enchanted our early childhood, those too who, during our long existence, have provided for us the happiest hours and the rarest of friends.

As a lover of nature once said: happy he who, resting in the grass in the evening close to an apiary, in the company of his dog, heard the song of the bees blending itself with the chirping of the crickets, with the sound of the wind in the trees, the twinkling of the stars and the slow march of the clouds!

The bee

The place of bees in nature

Animals, which are distinguished from plants through being able to move, are divided into two main categories: vertebrates and invertebrates.

The vertebrates, characterised by their vertebral column, comprising fish, batrachians, reptiles, birds and mammals, are of no interest here.

The invertebrates, those not having a vertebral column, have several branches: protozoa (infusoria), sponges, coelenterates (medusae, corals), echinoderms (sea urchins), worms (leeches, lumbricus), bryozoa, rotifers, molluscs (oysters, slugs, octopuses), arthropods and finally the chordata, which with their dorsal chord, form the transition between the invertebrates and the vertebrates.

It is the arthropods that interest us here.

The arthropods (from the Greek 'arthron', articulation, and 'ports, podos', foot) are also called *Articulata*. Their bodies show three distinct regions, head, thorax and abdomen. These are equipped with appendages: on the head the antennae and organs of mastication; on the thorax, the limbs.

Arthropods are divided into several classes: crustacea (lobsters), arachnids (spiders), myriapods (centipedes), insects or hexapods.

The insects (from Latin 'in', in, 'secare', cut), or hexapods (from Greek: 'hex', six, and 'pous, podos' foot) are characterised by always having six limbs. Insects breathe air.

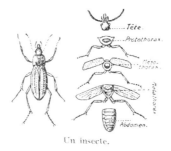

An insect

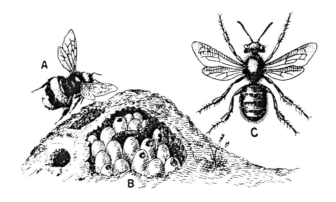

A: Bumble-bee, B: Bumble-bee nest, C: Osmia

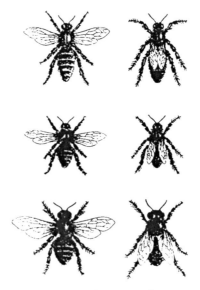

Top to bottom: A mother – a worker – a male

6

Their heads have two compound eyes. The thorax is divided into three parts, the prothorax which carries a pair of legs, the mesothorax which carries a pair of legs and a pair of wings, the metathorax which carries a pair of legs and sometimes a pair of wings. Insects always have the sexes separate. The larva after hatching from the egg undergoes a series of metamorphoses until it comes to resemble its parents. Because of their intelligence and organisation, insects are superior to other invertebrates. The 600,000 known species of insect are divided into eight orders: orthoptera (grasshoppers), neuroptera (ant-lions), odonata (dragonflies), hemiptera (bugs), diptera (fleas), lepidoptera (butterflies), coleoptera (cockchafers) and hymenoptera.

The hymenoptera (from the Greek 'humen', membrane, and 'pteron', wing) are characterised by four membranous wings,

Hymenoptera denotes the class of insects that is most highly organised from the point of view of intelligence, to such an extent that their manifestations overwhelm ours. And yet we still only have partial knowledge of their qualities, such as how many there are of them; for the 25,000 known species indicate that there may be as many as 250,000.

The hymenoptera comprise two groups: the sawflies and sting-bearers. The sawflies have an abdominal terebra for sawing or perforating plants. In this group is the class *Cephus*, in which is found the larva in the haulm which bears the ear of corn, and *Lydia piri*, whose larvae spin a kind of silk net enveloping several pear leaves.

The sting-bearers have a sting at the end of their abdomen. Some are parasites whose mission is often to destroy harmful insects, or carnivores like the common wasp or the hornet whose larvae need a supply of insects or meat, and the beewolf (*Philanthus triangulum*) which constantly rummages around on the ground to find larvae to feed on and which eats many bees.

The others are Formicoidea or ants, which, after the bees, are insects best endowed from the point of view of intelligence, and finally the Apides.

The Apides or honey-bearers are the bees. They feed their larvae on honey. There are about 1,500 species. Some are solitary, like *Osmia*, in holes in walls or in cavities of decaying timber. Others form social groups, such as the social bees including bumble-bees, stingless bees (*Melipona*) and the common bee or *Apis mellifera*.

The bumble-bees, large, very hairy insects, live only in small groups and make their nests below ground.

The *Melipona*, very small, live in large colonies, because they have several queens, and only in tropical countries.

The honey bee, *Apis mellifera*, is the one that we will be concerned with in greater detail.

Composition of the bee family

Bee families are called colonies. Each colony comprises three kinds of individuals:

1. A single, fully developed female capable of laying enough eggs to assure the maintenance and growth of the family. This is the mother, inappropriately called the 'queen';

2. The workers, or atrophied females, incompletely developed, a large number, 100,000 and more;

3. Some males, who only normally appear in the swarming season and disappear at the time when the nectar flow [also often referred to as 'honey flow', *Tr.*] ceases. Their number varies from a few hundred to a few thousand.

Comparative sizes

The mother, the workers and the males have different sizes. The table below gives the approximate sizes in millimetres:

	Length	Width of open wings	Diameter of thorax
Mother	16	24	4.0
Workers	12	23	3.5
Males	15	28	4.5

Comparative development

The hive inhabitants develop in different ways.

The queen spends three days at the egg stage, five as a larva and eight as a pupa (in a capped cell), hatching on the 16th day. She is fertilised around the seventh day after hatching. She begins to lay two days later, i.e. at least 25 days, more often 30 days, after the egg was laid.

The worker is three days at the egg stage, five days as a larva, and thirteen days as a pupa (in a capped cell). She hatches on the twenty-first day. She stays in the hive as a nurse or wax producer for about 15 days. She begins to forage thirty or thirty six days after the egg was laid.

The male spends three days at the egg stage and six and a half days as a larva, hatching on the 24th day. He is reproductively mature around the fifth day after hatching, i.e. about a month after the egg was laid.

N.B.

If the mother is removed from a colony, leaving it to the bees to replace her, to save time they almost always work with larvae aged two days, such that the young queens are ready on the twelfth day after removing the old queen.

The mother

The mother's name

Authors in antiquity taught that bee colonies were governed by a king. Today we know that in each colony there is a queen, or better, a mother, for, this mother is only a full female, fertilised and capable of assuring the future of her family through her laying. The overall ruler of the colony is the common interest. We shall however conform to common usage by calling the colony's mother 'queen'.

Number of queens

There is normally only one queen in a colony. Sometimes, however, we have seen two queens in a colony. Other beekeepers report having seen three. These exceptions happen for several reasons. A queen that is too old does not have sufficient energy to go and kill her daughter at birth, as earlier in her life her instinct would have driven her to do. Or possibly the beekeeper has introduced successively several queens to a colony he believed to be queenless. The queens have been kept separate, pushed by the bees in opposite directions. In fact they have formed different groups in the colony, each having the elements of one colony. This state disappears as soon as the groups become closer together, be it through the growth of the two groups, or through the arrival of cold weather. The disorder created by the departure of a secondary swarm favours for a while the presence of several hatched queens at the same time.

Antipathy of queens

When two queens meet, they attack one another. The strongest or the most able pierces the abdomen of the weaker one with its sting. Death is the result. Sometimes two queens sting each other, as happens to two duellists, and kill each other.

This antipathy exists between all mated queens, virgins, or even queens still enclosed in their cell.

When the bees raise queens for whatever reason, they make several queen cells, ten to fifteen. Now the queen that first hatches hurries to find the cells where her sisters are preparing to hatch, and pierces them with her sting.

I observe here a means of rigorous selection given by nature to the bee. Only one queen is saved out of ten or fifteen. For this queen is the one who was the first to lift the cover of her cell; she is the most vigorous.

Disappearance of the queen

During visits to hives one frequently sees very tight clumps of bees. If one separates them by force, or by heavy smoking, one finds a queen in the middle. Such a queen is said to be balled.

This embrace of the bees is caused by joy or antipathy.

When a beekeeper has kept a queen separated from her colony for too long, when he has not enabled a queen to leave her introduction cage quickly enough, or when there is robbing and danger for the queen, the bees in their excessive excitement press themselves round the queen as hard as they can, squeezing her, clasping her and suffocating her.

At other times this is caused by antipathy; it is accompanied by stings and a rapid death follows.

This happens to old infertile queens, shortly after the hatching of their successor; to queens that the beekeeper has kept too long between his fingers or hands, thus changing the particular scent that enables the workers to recognise her; and to young queens who on returning from mating, enter a foreign hive that is too near their own.

Consequences of the disappearance of the queen

A colony deprived of its queen is described as queenless. If the queen disappears and is not replaced by the beekeeper or the bees, the population of the colony diminishes rapidly until it disappears.

The importance of the queen

Her presence is necessary because only the queen lays the eggs destined for perpetuating the family. Nature too has taken all possible measures to keep her alive.

The queen is mated in the air during flight. These circumstances make this act dangerous for an insect as fragile as a bee. It is also unique.

The queen bee meets the male only once in her life. And subsequently never leaves her combs unless in the midst of a swarm that is leaving to start a new home.

Life-span of a queen

A queen lives from four to five years. This is about 50 times longer than the life-span of workers born at the beginning of the nectar flow. As with chickens, it is in the second year that she lays most prolifically.

Age of the queen

It is quite easy to distinguish old from young queens. Young queens in their first or second year have a larger abdomen, because it is distended with eggs, their wings are intact, their head and body are covered with hairs, and their movements are agile. Old queens of three years are smooth; their wings are damaged and their movement is slow.

Power of the queen

It is a mistake to believe that the queen directs the construction of the combs and shares out the work to the workers. The role of the queen is just to lay eggs.

It is nonetheless true that the presence of the queen is indispensable to the activity of the colony. The importance of the role of the queen and the seriousness of her loss is seen when a hive becomes queenless. The workers become agitated, roused, running in all directions in search of the queen. They work less and become bad tempered. The situation gets still worse if there is no young brood in the hive to allow raising a new queen.

Furthermore, in a colony that is dying of hunger, it is the queen who survives the longest, doubtless because the queen is stronger and more robust, but also because the bees save for her the last mouthful of honey.

Imperfections of the queen

The queen does not possess wax secreting organs nor the equipment for gathering pollen or honey.

The queen does not even know how to feed herself. If she is enclosed alone in a box with some honey within reach she will die of hunger beside the honey.

It seems to be the same in the hive. While she is laying, the workers supply the queen with brood food, a mixture of honey and pollen already modified by an initial digestion; and when she is not laying, pure honey. However, according to Dr. Miller, it is not the worker that passes the food into the mouth of its mother, because the discharge of the food is only possible with the tongue retracted. On the contrary, it is the queen who introduces her tongue into the mouth of the worker to take into her crop the brood food that is already prepared for her.

Character of the queen

The queen is shy and retiring. The slightest unusual noise frightens her. She often hides herself in the recesses of the hive where one might crush her, or at least have difficulty finding her. The queen does not even use her sting except against young queens.

Appearance of the queen

The queen's appearance makes it easy to find her. She is fatter and much longer than a worker. Her abdomen, of a lighter shade, extends well beyond her wings. Her deportment is more stately. She is distinguished equally from the male by her more slender body. The male has a much more rounded and hairier end to his abdomen. His wings are longer than his abdomen.

How to find the queen

In the People's Hive (Warré Hive) with a queen excluder we have a mechanical means quickly to find the queen without endangering her, and without the beekeeper being particularly experienced.

In framed hives there is another method for quickly finding a large number of queens, each day of the warm season, that has always worked well in our breeding work.

In the laying season, the queen appears each day to cross the space occupied by the brood in order to lay in all the empty cells and extend the brood according to the space available. At midnight the queen should always be at the centre. In any case, at midday the queen is always at one extremity of the brood, one day to the right and the next day to the left. It is important in order not to make a mistake to avoid frightening the queen by too sudden movements or by too much smoke, and always to put the queen back on the comb where she was found. If the operation is not performed at midday, the queen will have moved as far from the edge of the brood nest as the time of the operation is from midday.

Certainty that the queen is present

Even without having seen her, one can be certain that the queen is in a nest if there is larval worker-brood, and better still if there are newly laid eggs and if the bees are coming and going, bringing pollen as they return.

Odour of the queen

It is said that the queen has a strong odour, smelling like melissa, particularly as the bees of the colony more or less take it on.

The males

The name of the males

The males are generally called drones on account of their noise in flight, louder than a bumble-bee and quite different. *'Faux bourdons'* (false bumble-bees), their name in French, distinguishes them from the *'bourdons'* (bumble-bees) of the field.

Details of the male

The males are blacker. The extremities of their bodies are hairier. The legs are without the apparatus for collecting pollen. They have no sting. They have a distinct odour.

Odour of males

At swarm time the males emit a stronger odour. This is a means for the young female to recognise them, more than by the noise they make in flight. Moreover, this odour allows the emergence of swarms to be predicted.

Habits of males

The males are gentle and peaceful. In the hive they seem to always be asleep. They only go out around midday and only during fine, warm weather. They sometimes move from one hive to another without the bees getting angry with them.

Number of males

In colonies in good heart, there can be up to three thousand drones.

Functions of males

All agree that the function of the males is to fertilise the young females. We share the view of certain beekeepers, that the males are also useful to maintain the heat necessary for hatching the brood at any given time. We shall discuss this issue when we speak of the means of reducing their number or eliminating them.

Life span of males

In temperate climates the males live only a few months. They appear at the beginning of the nectar flow. They are killed by the workers as soon as it ceases. They are retained for a time, even in winter, by a queenless colony.

Indication of the presence of males

The presence of plenty of males during the nectar flow seems to indicate that the colony is strong and will give a good harvest if the circumstances are favourable. On the other hand, the presence of males after the nectar flow indicates with certainty that the colony is in a poor state, that it is queenless or has only an exhausted queen.

The workers

Functions of the workers

The workers perform the tasks of construction and maintenance of the comb and the jobs of feeding. They raise the brood, guard the hive, clean it and ventilate it, etc.

There is no way of distinguishing the workers except by the functions they perform, be it nursing, foraging, wax-making etc. All the workers are destined to perform all the useful tasks of the colony without distinction, according to the seasons, the time and the circumstances. Only the young workers are exclusively occupied with the work inside the hive, as their bodies are not sufficiently developed to withstand inclement weather.

Times of sorties

It has been said that workers go out at any time of day in spring, only in the morning in summer, and never when it is raining or cold.

It is more correct to say that the workers go out when their occupation is possible, as often as they have some chance of finding nectar, pollen or propolis.

But the rain so greatly weighs down the worker that it prevents her flying, and below 8 °C, bees becomes sluggish.

In summer, workers look for nectar first and foremost. But the midday sun dries up the flowers.

In spring it is above all pollen that the workers forage for. But neither heat not cold completely halts production.

Some figures

A bee weighs about one tenth of a gramme. She can bring back half her weight, i.e. 0.05 g, though sometimes she brings back only 0.02 g. To bring in a kilogramme of nectar, it is necessary for the bee to make 50,000 trips or 50,000 bees to make one trip. A bee can make twenty trips a day of one kilometre return, bringing in 0.4 g nectar. The harvest of 1 kg of nectar thus represents more than 40,000 kilometres, i.e. more than the circumference of the Earth.

Life span of a worker

Workers can live a maximum of one year following queenlessness and a bad season, i.e. when workers have little activity.

In normal colonies in a good season, as a result of their incessant activity, workers live a maximum of two or three months, often only three or four weeks.

Habits of workers

Amongst the bees of the same colony one observes a unity and understanding to a degree of perfection that exists nowhere else. For all the bees have one and the same aim, one and the same ambition, namely the prosperity of the colony.

For the same reason, the workers challenge neighbouring bees. They examine them and, except in certain cases, when they have recognised that they are strangers they drive them away and often sting them to death, without realising that this act of violence causes their own death.

Bee polymorphism

The difference between a worker and a queen comes solely from the shape of the cell in which the larva develops and its nourishment. Who dares to affirm this?

If it is a question of only more or less complete development, one might accept the dominant influence of nourishment and environment. But there are divergences between queen and worker which cannot be attributed to the conditions and to the cradle. The worker possesses certain organs such as pollen baskets and wax secreting glands which are missing on the queen, and she, for her part, has certain things that one does not find on the neuter bee. But this dissimilarity of the organism cannot be attributed to the conditions. It can only come from the nurse bees who by instinct know to what treatment they must subject a larva out of which will come a worker that will be endowed with the necessary organs for functions that she will have to fulfil; they know equally what upbringing to give a larva destined to produce a queen in order to fortify her or atrophy organs she does not need, and on the other hand develop those necessary for her maternal functions.

We have to admit that the nurse bees of a hive have an amazing ability if we wish to explain the polymorphism of the bees.

What can be seen in the surroundings of an apiary

When the temperature is favourable for the nectar flow, it is easy to follow the work of the bees, whether in a field or on the edge of a wood, and without danger of being stung, for as we have said, away from the hive the bee never stings.

We might even come to recognise our own bees, whether it be because they are a subspecies which does not occur in that region, or because on their leaving the hive we have dusted them with a powder of some kind, flour perhaps.

Nectar

Above all it is nectar that bees seek in the flowers. On arriving at a flower the bee parts the petals and plunges her head into the interior of the flower, extends her tongue and absorbs the droplet of nectar that we would have been able to see before she arrived.

Bee foraging on a flower

The bee moves immediately to another flower and repeats the process.

It is to be noted that the more abundant the nectar the more foragers there are; that in the same sortie the bee appears to go to a single species of flower; that the bee prefers some species to others, and that she ignores a flower visited previously by another bee.

The bee gathers nectar only from flowers, but also sometimes from the rest of the plant, for example from the stipules of vetch, and, in a warm season, sometimes from the leaves of oak, birch, beech, poplar, lime, etc. Such nectar is called honeydew.

Pollen

The bees also gather pollen which they use to feed the larvae. The foragers who gather nectar may also collect a certain amount of pollen, possibly involuntarily, but it is known that some workers collect pollen without nectar.

The bees take the pollen with their mandibles and press it into a ball and take that with their front legs to pass it into the baskets in their hind legs.

In certain flowers, such as broom or pink, there is so much pollen that the body of the bee is totally covered with it.

Pollen of more than one colour is never seen being carried by a single bee. It thus appears that the bee at each sortie visits just one species of plant to gather pollen. For the colour of pollen varies from species to species.

Propolis

Foragers also collect propolis from the buds of certain trees, for example alder, poplar, birch, willow, elm, etc.

Propolis is a resinous, transparent, sticky material. The bees bring it in the form of small pellets in the same way as pollen. They use it to plug the cracks and fill the voids in the interior of the hive.

Water

Finally, certain foragers also go to look for water which they use to dilute the paste for the young bees and probably also for dissolving crystallised honey.

The bees have strange preferences: drops of morning dew, seawater, stagnant water which has received liquid manure in the vicinity of farms.

What can be seen at the hive entrance

When the temperature allows, we can see males or drones and workers at the entrance of a hive.

Drones

The drones go out only during the warm hours of the day. They are noisy and fly aimlessly and heavily though carrying nothing, neither nectar nor pollen.

Workers

If the temperature is above 8 °C, we see workers always busy at the hive entrance, but doing different things. Some are guarding or fanning for ventilation, others are cleaning or foraging.

Guards

The guards come and go at the entrance of the hive. They scrutinise the bees coming in from outside and only let them enter after they have been recognised, doubtless by their odour. They chase away bees, however similar, coming from another hive to take their honey. They also chase away wasps, hornets and hawk moths which sometimes try to get into the hive.

Fanners

Towards evening on warm days, above all if there has been nectar brought in, beside the guards, the fanners stand firm with their heads pointing towards the entrance, erect on their legs. Their wings move rapidly producing a sound that one can hear at quite some distance. Their task is to ventilate the hive to lower the temperature and to increase the evaporation of the water contained in the newly gathered nectar.

Cleaners

In the morning, especially in spring, bees are seen leaving the hive carrying wax debris and dead bees far away. These are the cleaners.

Foragers

Finally we see the foragers emerging from the hive. They take to the air rapidly, without hesitation, in a definite direction, remembering flowers last visited. They return ponderously and sometimes fall in the grass surrounding the hive because they are laden with nectar. Others return carrying on their hind legs two balls of pollen, yellow or various other colours, that they have gathered from the stamens of flowers.

Orientation

On warm days, especially after several days of rain, one often sees bees flying in ever increasing circles round the hive. These are not foragers but young bees carrying out a reconnaissance of their hive and its position. This exercise is called 'orientation'.

In front: a cleaner bee bringing out a dead bee. In the middle: two drones, shorter and fatter.
Near the entrance: two workers carrying pollen that can be seen on their legs.

16

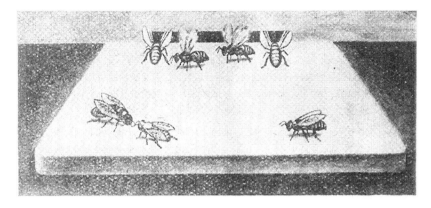

In front: a guard bee examining another bee. Near the entrance: ventilator bees fanning the hive.

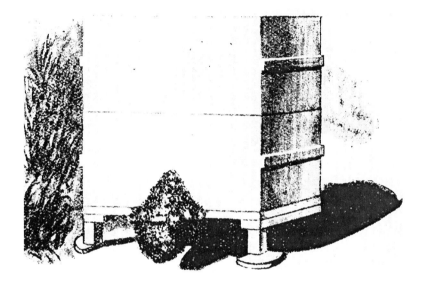

Bees making a beard

Beard

When it is very hot, the bees, lacking space in the hive to spread themselves out, pour out of the hive in a group in front of the entrance and even go under the hive, attached to each other by their legs. We say then that the bees make a beard. They form beards too when they are preparing to swarm.

What can be seen inside a hive

Comb

The first thing we notice inside a hive is the sheets of wax hollowed out with regular cavities. These sheets are called combs. The cavities are called cells or alveoli. Some are just started and others are finished. The combs are separated by about a centimetre.

Cells

The cells have different sizes. Cells of males are bigger; those of workers, smaller.

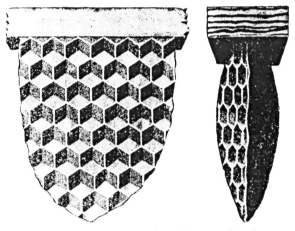

Combs under construction, face view and side view

There are also some irregular cells called transition cells. Finally there are sometimes some queen cells of a special shape outwardly resembling a peanut.

Eggs and larvae

Queen cells
Top: unfinished cells, c.
below it a cell whose queen
has emerged normally,
next, a capped cell containing
a queen, b. bottom: a torn cell
whose queen has been killed, d.

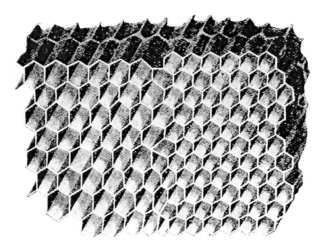

Left: drone cells. Right: worker cells. Middle: transition cells.

The cells may have a cover called a 'capping'. Cells that are not capped may be empty or may contain eggs, larvae, pollen or honey. Capped cells contain brood if the capping is domed and matt, honey if the capping is flat and bright.

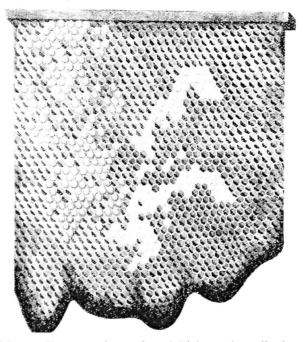

Left: capped drone cells, matt and more domed. Right: worker cells, domed and matt.

The eggs are horizontal on the first day, inclined on the second and resting on the base of the cell on the third. The newly emerged larvae vary in fatness according to their age.

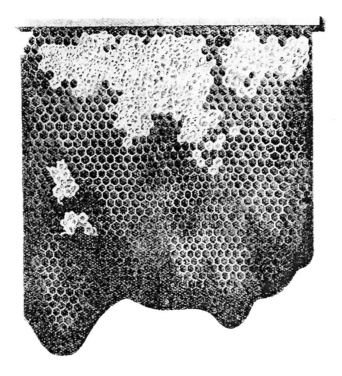

Top: capped cells containing honey; capping: flat and bright.

Occupants

In the hive there is of course a queen, some workers and some males. We have discussed them in a preceding chapter.

The queen has no task other than to lay. The workers are busy with various tasks: feeding the queen and the larvae; fetching nectar, pollen, propolis and water; cleaning the cells of the hive. The males are scattered on the brood with no apparent occupation, probably to warm it. If the hive is visited during hot periods, the males are outside or in the corners of the hive so as not to obstruct the workers.

The problems of beekeeping

It cannot be denied that beekeeping is a useful and pleasant activity.

So why is it not more developed? For bees are not in all the places where there are flowers to be fertilised and nectar to be gathered; or at least not enough of them.

The first problem is the bee's sting. The complexity of both beekeeping material and methods are another. Finally, the main problem is that the benefit appears too small to allow the practice of beekeeping.

But we are writing this book in order to remove all these obstacles. We tell you of the gentleness of the bee. We give you the measurements of an economically profitable hive. We show you a simple method that is at the same time economical. If you follow our advice, we guarantee that you are sure to get a good profit.

Beekeeping without stings

The first obstacle to the further spread of beekeeping is the bee's sting.

We can discuss bees for hours in any country in all classes of society. Everywhere and always we find attentive ears. Bees are friendly, but the best friends of bees avow that they do not keep bees because they fear the bee's sting. This sting does indeed seem formidable. But is it really so?

The bee is often maltreated, jostled by reapers or by animals when it forages in a meadow. But it never stings them.

Try the following experiment: when your trees are in flower, examine the bees foraging on these flowers. If you like, in order to better distinguish them, throw a little wheat or rice flour on one of them and follow her. Push her aside with a finger; she goes to another flower. Push her again and she moves further off. You can continue this game as long as you wish. The bee only gets angry when she has collected her load of nectar. She never stings you.

You may have seen professional beekeepers working in the midst of their bees, without fear, with no apparent precautions, without even covering their heads with a veil.

In the first editions of my book, I reproduced numerous photographs of all the annual beekeeping activities, including driving bees from a skep, a job that ends in hitting it with sticks. Now it can be seen from these photos that there are bees in the hives in question; that the operators are wearing neither gloves nor a veil; that they have as their sole weapon a modest Bingham smoker; and finally, at the foot of each open hive, there is my dog sitting peacefully, my dear friend Polo, a cocker spaniel with long ears and long hair, i.e. it has everything needed for just one bee to create mayhem if it was dissatisfied. One of these photos is reproduced here.

Thus, bees are not bad by nature.

But bees have the job of creating a family and making it prosper, collecting nectar and preserving it. And to defend the family and the honey it has received a powerful weapon, the sting with its venom. It uses it against all enemies, real or apparent, with a speed that nobody would know how to escape from, and with a force against which neither veils, nor gloves, nor gaiters, nor the thickest clothes can give protection.

As the beekeeper, however, provides his bees with a suitable home, sufficient stores, and as he presents himself to them as a friend, he will be well accepted by the bees, and after a few moments of communion, he may without danger shake his good bees, jostle them, even brush them aside as we do frequently.

I do not know of a single other animal that one can treat so roughly as the bee.

I would say that there are two types of person who are at risk of being frequently stung by bees. They are first of all violent people, violent in their gestures and violent in their words. Then there are people who have a strong smell, whether pleasant or not. For example: people having foetid breath – as the smell comes from bad dentition, or an upset stomach or from alcoholism; or people who are dirty, or perfumed. But everyone else may keep bees with the certainty of not being stung by them, on one condition only, that they are never allowed to suspect that they are the enemies of their keeper. Now this should be an easy matter for those who wish to follow my method, each operation of which I will describe to you in a precise way, and will detail the manner of proceeding.

Despite my affirmations on the gentleness of bees, I accept that certain people are sometimes insurmountably apprehensive when it comes to approaching bees with their face uncovered. This is why, with my method, I provide for using a veil, which gives the beekeeper the assurance that they cannot be stung on the face.

Furthermore, my method reduces or eliminates the risk of stings. Driving the bees from one hive to another is done at some distance from the apiary. During this operation one cannot therefore be approached by bees from neighbouring hives or foragers of the hive being transferred. No comb is removed from the hive with the bees present. The beekeeper therefore cannot squash or irritate the bees. During the routine tasks of the year the hive is opened once, at the harvest. There is therefore no frequent chilling of the brood chamber, i.e. no cause for irritating the bees.

You may therefore carry out beekeeping without danger of being stung. I do not hesitate to say that when a beekeeper is stung by his bees he should always ask what mistake he has made.

The choice of hive

The second difficulty for the novice beekeeper is choosing a hive, i.e. knowing how he is going to house his bees.

There are many different systems of hive and all have their enthusiasts and opponents.

This difficulty can be overcome. And here is how.

Do not try to experiment

It is not unusual to hear the novice deciding as follows: 'I will try out two or three of the most fashionable systems, study them, and see which is best'.

But life is short, especially active life. Unless you are especially privileged, you will not be able to reach a definite conclusion.

To test different hives, they need to be studied in the same apiary, under the same management, with a minimum of between ten and twelve hives in each system, over a period of ten years. Put another way, it is necessary that these hives be in an identical situation and that they will give a true average.

But after these ten years they may observe that a particular system is perfect in winter, for example, and another is better in summer. They will thus devise a single hive system that combines all the advantages of the two systems studied previously. And they will study this new hive system for another ten years. After this second study they may realise that they have a hive that is perfect for the bees, answering all their needs, but poor for the beekeeper because it needs far too much attention. Would they then try a new ten-year experiment? Could they?

As amateurs do such experiments, they get great satisfaction. Such experiments have provided even myself with many enjoyable hours.

Those who wish to produce, or have to, would do well to avoid them.

Hive systems studied in my apiaries: 1. Duvauchelle hive. 2. Voirnot hive, semi-double, run as two colonies of eight frames. 3. 10-frame Voirnot hive. 4. Dadant-Blatt hive. 5. Layens hive, run as two colonies of 9 frames with a super. 6. 12-frame Layens hive with a super.

Hive systems studied in my apiaries (continued): 7. 9-frame Layens hive. 8. 12-frame Jarry hive, warm-way. 9. 30x40, shallow, 10-frame Congrès hive. 10. 30x40, shallow, 8-frame Congrès hive. 11. The people's hive [Warré hive, *Tr.*] with moveable frames. 12. The people's hive with fixed comb (one of the prototypes).

Question the advice of others

Of course, beekeepers, whether writing or speaking, recommend the hive that they have chosen, or the one that they have invented, as they believe that they have perfected it. But paternal love is blind. Beekeepers do not see the defects of their hives. They mislead you without realising it.

One passion drives humanity, namely vanity. Let us call it self-love.

But self-love prevents the beekeeper admitting that he is mistaken in his choice of hive, unless he happens to discover it himself. He will say that it gives excellent results. And by force of repeating this, perhaps he will end up convincing himself. And without thinking he is deceiving you, he will promise you amazing harvests. In fact you will be deceived.

It is also necessary to recognise that sometimes personal interest guides certain beekeepers. They do not want the competition to increase, so they recommend what they disdain.

Hive manufacturers, on the other hand, will be motivated to recommend the hive that they mass produce. It gives them more profits. It is not always the best. It is thus better not to listen to anyone. It is just as well that there is an infallible means of recognising the best hive.

Base yourself on apicultural or scientific principles which everyone accepts and that no one will argue with.

The value of my advice

For more than thirty years I have studied in my apiaries the main hive systems shown in the illustrations reproduced here.

I have in my apiaries 350 hives of different systems. I have been able to make comparisons.

However, I do not wish to impose my experience on anyone. To appraise my hive and method, the fruit of my researches, I will not impose myself, my work nor the results obtained. I will simply give you the reasons for their superiority, reasons based on incontestable apicultural and scientific principles.

Furthermore, even when I give the dimensions of the hive that I recommend, my advice has absolutely no personal interest.

The best hive

Scientific beekeeping

Do you wish to study the bee while it is living and going about its work? To do this, you will not only need a hive with windows, but also one that you can study at will in all its nooks and corners. In this case, it is the framed hive that is needed, and also the frames of this hive should be moveable at will. It is necessary that the frames be 'openable', like the pages of a book.

It is a hive of this kind that François Hubert used for his famous observations.

This hive is expensive and there is no profit from it.

It is a sacrifice for science.

Productive beekeeping

On the other hand, would you like to obtain from your hive honey that is guaranteed natural and less costly than that at the grocers? Would you like to start a cultural activity that nourishes you and your family? In this case, you will need a hive that is less expensive, a hive whose management demands less work from you, whose honey simply costs less. Then only a hive with fixed combs will give you this result.

Reasons for this advice

This advice might appear rash in view of the large number of framed hives of all systems that are on offer and used by beekeepers.

Reflect on this fact. Which are the modern hives that have not been abandoned after some years of experience? Those of schoolteachers, of vicars, etc. who have spare time not devoted to other things. And those of beekeepers who have known and been able to combine with their apiary some kind of business such as constructing hives, making confectionery, etc.

All the other apiaries disappear quickly because they do not feed their owner.

Moreover, it is not necessary to make a comparative study of modern hives to account for their lack of value. It would be costly, as we have said. It is sufficient to calculate what it costs to install them, what time is required in their management in order to be able to conclude, without even being a beekeeper, that their product necessarily costs too much. The cost of framed hives and their accessories can be found in the catalogues of the manufacturers. We will not take up our time with them. We shall only consider the number of hours' work that each system requires.

Number of systems

The number of types of hive continues to increase. They remove a centimetre here and add one there. They take the frames through all geometric forms and advertise a new hive which will assure, better than others, that the beekeeper will make a fortune. This begins by increasing the capital outlay, as all these modifications generally increase the cost of the hive. In any case, they do not constitute a new system because they are not based on an essential apicultural principle.

But many beekeepers are obsessed with invention. They have to change something on the hives that they own.

Even the People's Hive [Warré Hive, *Tr.*] has already been a victim of the inventors. They say they are improving it. But the improvements I have heard of are useless, some are harmful, and a few absurd.

In fact all the commercial hives can be divided into four systems: the Dadant hive, the Voirnot, the Layens and the skep.

The Dadant hive

Ch. Dadant (from *L'Apiculteur*)

The Dadant hive contains 12 frames. The frames have the following measurements: depth, 266 mm; length, 420 mm; its supers have half-frames.

Its popularity

As soon as it appeared the Dadant hive became a great success.

A very disillusioned person said of the French: 'Wantonness, inconstancy, desire for novelty and fashion, that they follow blindly in not only the most serious, but also the most frivolous matters'. A diplomat put it: 'The French are big babies who accept without hesitation what someone else says, above all a stranger'.

And a historian wrote: 'The French have a mania for praising what comes from outside, at the expense of what they have at home'.

For, although Dadant was French by birth, he was living in America. Moreover, the Dadant hive that we use is not the one that Dadant used. And Dadant was more a manufacturer of foundation than a beekeeper. Nobody is concerned about this.

Furthermore, the Dadant hive offers something for the entrepreneur. Businesses were started and proliferated. They all ordered the Dadant hive that made them a living. With the skep they had hardly any fittings to make for it.

Finally it should be recognised that the Dadant allowed the use of the extractor, an invention whose usefulness is undeniable. It was not foreseen that with a few modifications the extractor could be used to extract honey from hives with fixed comb.

Its measurements

The measurements of the Dadant hive clearly requires more wood than a hive of 300 x 300 mm. Wood is expensive.

In addition, in spring when the colony wants to expand its brood nest, it has to warm the hive over a (horizontal) surface area of 2,000 cm^2 instead of 900 cm^2 as in our hive. Yet honey is the bee's sole combustible material. The bee is overworked by the increased surface to warm and an additional consumption of winter stores results.

Its frame

Some people regard the frame as essential to monitoring the hive, for treating disease and for extracting honey.

But I regard frames as one of the main causes of disease. In facilitating visits to the inside of the hive it increases such visits which exhausts the bees in re-establishing the hive temperature, weakening the colony and increasing its chance of contracting disease. There is no need for frames to assess the state of the stores. If in autumn one leaves the necessary stores, there is no further need to bother about them.

There is no need for frames to check the state of the colony. If the bees are bringing in pollen, there is a queen and brood. All is well.

The number of arrivals and departures indicate the strength of the colony.

If there is a large drop in the number of sorties, it is best to do away with the colony and replace it with a swarm or with driven bees. If, in this process, you notice a bad smell or decomposition of the brood, it is necessary to disinfect the hive with a flame or bleach. This is more economical than all the advocated treatments, which are suitable only for experts who carry out research.

No more is there need for frames to extract the honey. We have cages which allow extraction of fixed comb by means of an extractor. With these cages, the fixed comb stays put and does not break. In these respects the performance is at least as good as with frames.

And then the frame enthusiasts have to ask themselves: how long does the framed hive keep its mobile frames after they have left the joinery workshop? Two years at most. For most beekeepers do not do spring-cleaning and the frames are soon stuck to each other and to the inner surfaces of the hive. So why use frames?

In any case, as with all frames, the Dadant frame requires a finely planed finish to facilitate its cleaning at the spring visit. In addition, it demands a high degree of precision in manufacture. It is necessary to leave a space of 7.5 mm between the inside walls of the hive and the frames, and to keep it like this. If the space falls to 5 mm the bees fill it with propolis. If the space is 10 mm the bees construct comb in it, because they abhor empty space. In both cases the frames cease to be mobile. The required precision increases the capital cost of the hive.

Furthermore, the Dadant hive has a long, shallow frame shape. Eighteen kilos of honey distributed between 12 frames hardly provides one kilo for the frames at the middle. There will even be honey only in the corners and none at the centre. The wintering bees cluster on the honey at the corners, at the front or rear of the hive, on the sunny side. When they have consumed all the honey above their cluster, they move to the other extremity of the frame where there is still some honey. But if the temperature is low, they will not be able to make this move because they will not find in the middle of the frames the necessary provisions to make the journey. They will die of hunger where they are, yet with stores nearby. This is a big disadvantage of hives with frames that are shallow and long.

Finally, the frame considerably increases the hive volume. We have already indicated the disadvantage of this.

Wax foundation

Wax foundation used in the Dadant hive is expensive. The accessories that it requires are expensive. Inserting this foundation is fiddly and takes time. Foundation is thus a considerable consumer of time and money and increases the capital cost of the hive, and as a result, the honey.

But outside the nectar flow, foundation brings very minimal return, it economises only a very small amount on honey, and still less on time, for the bees do not always leave the cells in the state in which they have been given to them.

During the nectar flow, the only time when the comb can be drawn, foundation is more harmful than useful. The wax is nothing other than the sweat of the bee. And during the nectar flow, bees sweat a lot, because they always put the most effort into their work. Foundation is thus useless at this time, and even harmful as it prevents bees from constructing their comb vertically and evenly.

The frame, fitted with foundation, immediately placed in the hive, brings about a heat differentiation from its bottom to its top.

It follows that the various distortions of the foundation and the steel wire supporting it result in warping in the comb. Without foundation, the bees construct their combs according to their needs, with the best wax (their own) and with the normal thickness of a comb. They thus strengthen it as they extend it.

This is the reason why we do not use foundation. We are satisfied with placing a starter of 5 mm of unadulterated, raw wax.

And we do not consider this starter as a saving in honey, but as a means of encouraging the bees to construct their combs in the same direction in order to make it easier for the beekeeper.

Populating the hive

To populate a Dadant hive a swarm of 2 kg is insufficient, still less one of 1.5 kg. It is necessary to use a swarm of 4 kg. This is not commercially available. A swarm of 2 kg requires two years to settle in and give a harvest. In our hive a 2 kg swarm settles in in the first year and gives a harvest three months after hiving.

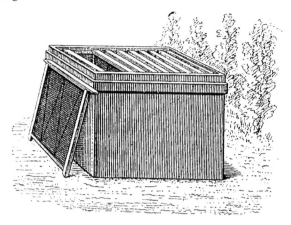

Modern hive: one of the frames, fitted with wax foundation, is removed from the hive.

Its boards

The brood chamber of the Dadant hive is covered with boards or oilcloth. But in any hive there is humidity caused by the evaporation of nectar and animal respiration. And this humidity, heated by the bee cluster, rises to the top of the hive, stops at the boards, cannot pass through them, spreads to the sides of the hive where it cools, falls as a mist on the outside frames, and damages their combs. Whence a loss. This mist keeps the bees in an atmosphere that is constantly humid. It is not healthy. Our covering over the combs avoids this loss and looks after the health of the bees.

Its quilt

The quilt that covers the brood chamber of a Dadant hive is only between three and four centimetres deep and comprises a cloth above and below. This thickness is insufficient for the quilt to fulfil its role as an insulator. Furthermore, the cloth over it prevents one from seeing if its contents are still insulating, for sooner or later the dampness stops it doing so. We prefer our quilt of 10 cm uncovered. It is more efficient and the replacement of its contents is easier and quicker.

The spring visit

It is necessary to open Dadant hives, as indeed all the framed hives, in spring, in April in the region of Paris, from midday to 2 p.m., and during good weather.

For it is important that the colony is not too well developed, or the temperature too low. The outside temperature is always lower than that of the hive. This is why it is recommended that one proceeds rapidly, albeit without roughness.

In this opening of the hive, it is first of all necessary to clean all the frames and the inside walls. Then all the old frames should be removed. Bees abhor empty space.

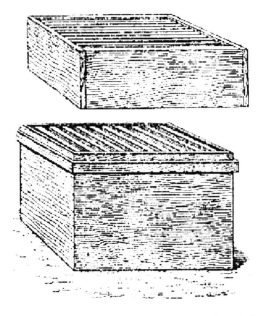

Modern hive and its super (shallow box). Bottom: brood chamber.

The bees strive continuously to fill the gaps even between the combs and the sides of the hive. If this propolis, as much on the frames as on the walls, is not removed each year from the first year onwards, manipulation of the frames becomes difficult, and becomes impossible in the second or third year.

When the hive is first opened at the spring visit it is necessary therefore to take out the frames one by one and scrape them all round to remove the propolis.

The frames also have to be moved aside to scrape the walls of the hive. After this procedure one has to take out all the old, black frames. In the old frames, the cells are reduced in size by the cocoons left by each bee when it hatches. If these old frames are kept, the bees hatching from them will become smaller and smaller, weaker at their work, and incapable of resisting disease. Now, these frames sometimes contain brood. It is therefore necessary to remove them, put them further away from the centre, await hatching and return later to remove them.

This work annoys the bees whose young are cooled, requires the bees to consume stores to re-warm the brood chamber, and calls for a considerable outlay of time by the beekeeper. Also, we do not hesitate to point out that an individual beekeeper does not manage to carry out this intervention every year in forty hives.

But our method reduces the spring visit to an insignificant job, which, moreover, can be done at any time or temperature, because it does not involve opening the hive. It is worth noting here that the hives said to be automatic are not really automatic except in the joinery workshop. At the apiary they are no longer so.

Its expansion

Whereas in winter the volume of a hive should be reduced to a sufficient minimum, in summer it should provide the bees with a space sufficiently large to develop the colony, and for the incoming nectar. This means adding supers (shallow boxes). But in order to avoid chilling the brood and stopping laying, we should not put the supers on too soon. And in order to avoid swarming and reduction of the harvest, we should not put them on too late either. In principle we can put a super on when all the frames except one at each side of the brood chamber are occupied. It is often necessary to add a second super when the first is three quarters full with honey. Thus it is necessary to open the hives to assess the situation. Yet the hives are not all at the same stage of development. We thus have to open the hives several times, resulting in time being expended, chilling the brood chamber, consumption of stores and stressing and annoying the bees.

However, in our method, we place the additional boxes *underneath* and not on top of the brood chamber and without opening the hive. We can put several there at the same time and as soon as we wish, even when making our spring visit, and whatever the outside temperature. A great economy of time is the consequence.

Its stores

In view of its size and the inspections it requires, the Dadant hive needs 18 kg stores for winter. Some authors say 20 kg.

In our hive 12 kg stores are sufficient. The difference is considerable.

After the above presentation, a knowledge of beekeeping is not necessary to understand that in the management of the Dadant hive, the bee is ceaselessly thwarted in its intentions, ceaselessly forced into an over-exertion that is not provided for by nature, and to consume honey wastefully. Thus the bee becomes more irritable. She also becomes less resistant to disease and the beekeeper wastes several kilogrammes of honey and a lot of time.

The Voirnot hive

Abbé Voirnot (from *L'Apiculteur*)

Abbé Voirnot must have known the two good French hives, Decouadic and Palteau. He could have been able as successfully as I was to find a way of using the extractor to extract the fixed combs of these hives. His knowledge and perseverance in other researches showed he was equal to the work.

But Abbé Voirnot never spoke of these two hives. Fascinated by the advantages of the extractor, he straight away accepted the framed hive which immediately enabled him to use the extractor.

But he did not accept the Dadant hive, as was presented to him. He understood its faults.

Size

The size of the Dadant hive excited everyone at first. After some very commendable observations, Abbé Voirnot concluded that 100 square decimetres of combs gives the hive the size that is necessary, yet sufficient for winter and spring. It is the size that he gave to his hive and which made it superior to the Dadant hive.

Depth and shape

Abbé Voirnot gave a greater depth to the frame of his hive so that the bees always had all their stores above their cluster. Thus no more death of colonies beside good stores.

Abbé Voirnot gave his hive a square shape, because this shape was closer to the shape of a cylinder, a shape in which the distribution of heat occurs more evenly, but whose construction is too expensive.

The square shape allows placement of the hive warm-way or cold-way as one wishes; a small advantage.

Abbé Voirnot also gave his hive a cubic shape, because this shape approaches a sphere, a shape in which the distribution of light occurs most evenly. Here Abbé Voirnot made a mistake. In a hive we do not have to allow for light; the bees want only darkness in it. And this cubic shape prevented Abbé Voirnot from promoting his frame as much as M. de Layens did his. An unfortunate mistake.

Expansion

Abbé Voirnot also saw the inconveniences of expansion in the Dadant hive. On this point he was content with reducing to 100 mm the depth of the super of his hive. It is a small matter.

Populating the hive and stores

In view of the size of the Voirnot hive, a swarm of 2 kg suffices to populate it, and between 15 kg and 16 kg of honey is sufficient as winter stores. These are two important advantages. But do not forget that in our hive, 12 kg stores generally suffices.

Apart from the advantages that we have indicated, the Voirnot hive retains all the faults of the Dadant hive including frames, foundation, quilt, spring visit, expansion, stores and boards.

The Layens hive

De Layens (from *L'Apiculteur*)

Like Abbé Voirnot, M. de Layens gave his frame a depth of 370 mm. This frame is better than that of the Voirnot hive, which is only 330 mm. With this frame, still better than with that of the Voirnot hive, the bees always have their stores above their cluster. No colony mortality next to plentiful stores there either. The Layens hive, reduced to 9 frames with partitions gives a perfect situation for wintering.

The Layens frame size of 370 x 310 mm approaches that of two combs one above the other of our hive 400 x 300 mm.

Populating the hive and stores

In the Layens hive, reduced to 9 frames with the partitions, a 2 kg swarm suffices, and between 15 kg and 16 kg of honey likewise as winter stores. Note that it is again between 3 kg and 5 kg more than with our hive.

Expansion

M. de Layens also saw great difficulties with placing the super on the Dadant hive. It is clear that he simply did away with the super and replaced it with additional frames at each side of the brood chamber. M. de Layens was mistaken. When the bees have filled the frame positioned next to the brood chamber with honey, they cannot pass across this frame to carry nectar to the subsequent frames. This frame has to be monitored. When it is half-filled with honey one has to move it back and put an empty frame in its place. Otherwise the bees swarm because of shortage of usable space. The difficulties of expanding are not decreased, on the contrary.

The Layens hive thus has as its only advantage the depth of its frame. Apart from that it has all the faults of the Dadant hive including frames, foundation, boards, quilt, spring visit, expansion and stores.

Observations

The Layens hive is referred to as modernised. But it is 50 years since we have abandoned this 9-frame hive with supers. It is good for wintering, but the bees rarely ascend to the supers. At the top of the deep frames there is often still a small amount of honey. But the bees are reluctant to cross the honey. They prefer to swarm.

The combination hive

Beekeeping without principles

I do not ignore the fact that many hive owners do not manage them according to the principles of apiculture that I have discussed.

They throw a swarm in a hive. In spring they add a super. In autumn they gather the honey from the super. That is all.

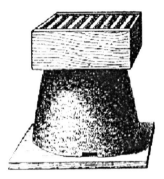

Combination hive with its super.

There is too much honey in the brood nest and the bees swarm in spring, lacking room. Or equally, there is not sufficient honey and the bees die of hunger if one does not save them soon enough with a terribly expensive feed.

The bees hatching in the old combs are weak, lack resistance to disease and are a risk to neighbouring apiaries.

Furthermore, the frames in the brood nest soon cease to be mobile.

Logical beekeeping

Modern hives would not suit such beekeepers. They should adopt the combination hive. The combination hive is a skep with fixed comb on which is placed a super with moveable frames. The bottom, or brood nest, may be made of straw, osier or wood.

The domed hive would suit them equally, but I strongly suggest that these hives have only one point in their favour, namely that they are cheap to set up, but they lead to disasters because their combs are not renewed and because the stores are not checked. If the stores are insufficient, the bees die. If the stores are too abundant, the bees swarm because they lack room. In any case, they go up neither into the super nor the dome, because they do not cross over the honey.

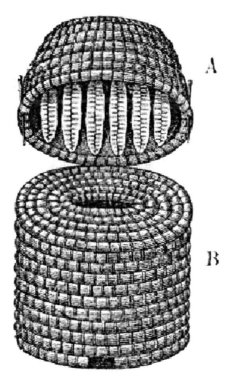

Domed hive: A – dome; B – hive body

The skep

Its enthusiasts

Many new amateur beekeepers adopt the modern hive for its frames and appearance. A good number of owners of skeps nevertheless remain faithful to their system.

The majority are wise country folk who prefer certainty, even probability. But the years pass without them seeing evidence of their mistake.

Here is an observation that leads to the same conclusion. In the village where I was born each family had its apiary.

Each winter, all my childhood friends ate an abundance of delicious bread and honey, just as I did. Twenty years later, I was the only person who had beehives. In some gardens, there was an abandoned Dadant or Layens hive, empty of course. The owners had let themselves be tempted by the advertisement of some on displays at agricultural shows. They believed they would do better with these modern hives. In fact they abandoned the only hive that suited them.

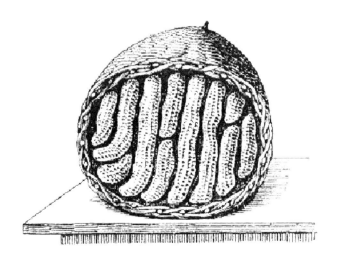

Interior of a skep

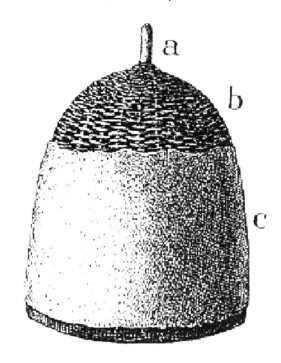

Osier skep: a – handle; b – thin wood; c – coating of daub (*pourget*: a mixture of clay and cow-dung).

Its methods

The methods used with skeps are as various as the aims pursued by the beekeepers. Moreover, these methods remain for the large part mysterious. It is very difficult to get to know them in detail.

In any case, here is what was done in my father's apiary, where there were always twelve or fifteen skeps.

The hives were made in the winter evenings, with rye straw, bound with split bramble or string.

Skep with hackle (straw roof)

Its volume was 40 litres. At their strongest, in the first spring, they received in the manner of a super, only underneath, the wooden ring of a kitchen sieve with the mesh removed. In autumn all the colonies of hives weighing more than 25 kg were suffocated (sulphured) and the honey and the wax harvested.

In the course of the summer the empty skeps received all the swarms. In spring, some slow colonies died of hunger. From them, the wax was harvested.

At my parents' home there was always plenty of honey for masters and workers, even for the farmyard animals. All our friends in the village also had their share each year.

Although this procedure was simple and cost little, it was barbarous, even unprofitable, and also irrational, as it did not produce the maximum yield. However, the procedure obtained honey cheaply, and healthy and strong bees to repopulate the modern hives that frequently died out.

A good method

In support of skeps, here is how it could be done: at the beginning of the main nectar flow, make the bees ascend into an empty skep as we describe later in the chapter 'Driving (transferring) bees'. Harvest the honey and wax and destroy the brood.

Let us be sensible

Various things make people turn to beekeeping: some from want of sugar, others from necessity of having some remunerative work. Some apiaries are set up. Some apiaries are extended. Small apiaries will certainly disappear because sugar will return on to the free market. There will nevertheless remain more hives than ever. There will thus be a greater production of honey.

But will actual consumption of honey be maintained? Yes, if honey is sold at the same price as sugar, i.e. on the whole cheaper, for sugar is the main competitor for honey. People do not buy honey instead of butter, but instead of sugar.

Honey is the only healthy sweetener, that is certain. But sugar has a stronger sweetening power and it is easier to handle.

The optimists tell us that the public, obliged to use honey for several years, have been able to appreciate its qualities and that they will remain faithful to it, and that clever publicity will continue to push the public towards honey. I do not believe any of this.

I have done a lot of publicity in my life, for both honey and medicinal plants. I have had correspondents not only in France but around the world, in Turkey, in India, in China, in America, etc., etc. And I have noticed that everywhere there are reasonable people who know how to submit to the laws of nature and health, to have a life without suffering and a late death without pain. Yes, but how few! The majority of people, the larger number, prefer a pill or injection to a cup of herb tea, a lump of sugar to a teaspoon full of honey, some for obvious reasons of economy, quite a lot because of convenience, many simply to do the same as everyone else. And like everyone else, they contract all possible kinds of illness; like everyone else, they provide a living for doctors and pharmacists; like everyone else, they die sooner and more painfully. Did not a wise man write that people eat themselves to death?

Have people learned from experience? I have not noticed it.

Thus beekeepers come to sell honey at the same price as sugar, and even cheaper if they wish to attract the new customers that they need.

Under these conditions, will beekeeping still be profitable? Yes, but on the condition that economical hives are used and an economical method is followed in order to obtain honey at a minimal cost of production. Certainly this result cannot be obtained with the hives and methods currently in vogue that we have already referred to. But it can with the method that we are going to present to you.

Origin of the People's Hive (Warré Hive)

Having decided to take up beekeeping I was bewildered by the diversity of systems of modern hives.

The Dadant hive was the most widespread. Firstly, it allowed use of the extractor, a very useful invention. But already the Voirnot and Layens hives, which were criticisms of it from different points of view, were significantly competing with it. Another hive started to appear. It was the Congrès hive, with 300 x 400 mm frames, in two forms, one shallow, the other deep. Not being able to draw a reasoned conclusion from the reverberating polemic in those days, I decided to adopt all these systems in order to study them.

In other respects, the studies of Abbé Voirnot on the volume of the hive seemed interesting to me, all the more so for Dr. Duvauchelle, my first mentor in beekeeping, modified his hive and gave it eight frames 300 x 400 mm (shallow), i.e. 96 square decimetres of comb. But the Voirnot hive has 100 square decimetres of comb. Dr. Duvauchelle thus appears to adopt Abbé Voirnot's conclusions on this point.

Previously, his hive had only 8 frames 280 x 360 mm, thus 81 square decimetres of comb.

Wishing to understand the basis of this issue of the volume of the hive during winter, I constructed hives with 9 Layens frames and hives with 8 frames 300 x 400, some deep and others shallow. These hives had a volume approximately the same as the Voirnot hive.

Not wishing to base my experiment on one or two hives, but on at least a dozen of each system, I had to make 350 hives.

To my great surprise, I noticed straight away that the bees consumed less of their stores in the hives with single walls where they would feel the cold still more in winter. This is however normal. In single-walled hives, the bees are torpid; they are as if in a continuous sleep. Now, who dines in that condition? With hives with warm walls, the bees are active for longer, and thus have need of sustenance. The single-walled hive thus economises on wood and stores, by as much as 2 kg from November to February. I also quickly noticed that in the brood chambers covered with boards or oilcloth, the end frames were quickly turning black and even rotting through the effect of the humidity. The same did not hold true in the brood chambers covered with canvas. We have given the reasons for this earlier.

After fifteen years of observations, I believed I could draw the following conclusions.

M. de Layens, the beekeepers' advocate, had reason to say that the Dadant hive demands too great an outlay of money and time; he created a good frame; he suggested a hive design that is easy and economical. On the other hand he took the wrong track in replacing the super with frames positioned horizontally against the brood.

Abbé Voirnot, the bees' advocate, was right when he said Dadant's hive harmed bees because of its volume and that of its super. Voirnot's hive was a great step forward.

I thus resolved to repeat the studies of these master beekeepers with the hope of reaching a better result, since, following on from their work, I would have the benefit of it.

Finally we can draw the following major conclusion: the volume of the Voirnot hive is sufficient, albeit smaller, therefore better, for the smaller the brood chamber the smaller is winter consumption of stores. However, wintering was better on deep frames like the Layens frame and the frame of 300 x 400 mm deep.

We preferred the 300 x 400 mm frame because it simplified our calculations.

Moreover, the shape of a hive of eight 300 x 400 mm frames approaches the shape of a swarm and allows the bees to put more honey above their cluster, which favours good wintering, even in cases of prolonged cold.

Furthermore, this shape facilitates the development of brood in spring. When the bees want to extend the brood downwards a centimetre, they have to heat this centimetre over all the surface of the hive. Now this surface varies from 900 cm^2 in our hive to 2,000 cm^2 in the Dadant hive. It is clear that the work of the bees will be easier in our hive.

And yet eight frames of 300 x 400 mm, in providing us with the necessary surface, gave a square shape. And the square is the shape that best approaches that of a cylinder, an ideal shape because it favours the distribution of the heat in the inside of the hive. But the cylinder is a shape that is hardly practicable.

The square shape also allows placement of the hives warm-way in winter and cold-way in summer, something to be considered.

I thus had a hive of eight 300 x 400 mm frames, a hive that was ideal for winter. But if the hive should be of reduced size in winter, in summer it should provide the bees with the space they need, generally two or three times more than in winter. How was this to be done?

Put a super on this hive? This was to fall back into the mistake attributed to the Dadant hive; time wasting and chilling the brood. In our case there was another disadvantage too. We had observed that the bees ascend with difficulty into supers placed above deep frames, because there remains a little honey at the top of these frames. And bees cross over honey with difficulty.

Place another hive-body box underneath as Abbé Voirnot did in his out-apiaries? For many hives, the result was good. The bees filled the upper hive with honey and installed themselves in the lower one. We lifted off the upper hive to harvest the honey and in spring we put it under the inhabited hive.

From this action, all beekeeping work became simpler. In spring, we started with cleaning the floor after having moved the hive without taking the top off. We neither cleaned the frames nor renewed the old comb. We did this work when each hive-body box came into our hands at the workshop, every two years.

Enlargement by one hive-body box placed under the other is also a big step forward. It is unnecessary to uncover the hives to see what they need. This enlargement can be done very early, without danger of chilling, in order to avoid swarming with greater certainty, and, for all hives, weak or strong.

However, the bees did not always fill the top hive-body box with honey. There was sometimes some brood at the bottom of the frames and some honey at the top. Harvesting was difficult. And my helpers frequently said: 'We ought to be able to saw this box in two'.

We have replaced it with two boxes giving the same volume with the same shape. We did the same with the one below. We harvested the boxes full of honey at the top, one or two, and left the following two boxes for wintering. We took away the others if necessary. In spring we placed one or more boxes underneath.

At a convenient time we raised queens and supplied swarms. But one evening, an order for 12 swarms was cancelled. I had empty hives to put them in, but I had only enough foundation for two hives. I settled for putting starters in the others as raw wax at the top of the frames, helped greatly by my knife in putting these starters in order. And I noticed that on these starters the bees constructed their combs as quickly as those on foundation and that these combs were more regular. I thus decided to continue to use only starters of raw wax and I have never come to regret it.

The People's Hive was thus designed.

And if small hives with frames economise on winter stores and facilitate the development of brood in spring, a hive with fixed comb will do it better because its volume is smaller: 36 litres instead of 44. We therefore designed the People's Hive with fixed comb. Now we noticed that the People's Hive with fixed combs saved an extra 3 kg of stores compared with the People's Hive with frames. We thus had two hives: the People's Hive with fixed comb, a perfect hive, but not convenient on a commercial scale because it does not allow the extractor to be used, and the People's Hive with frames, very superior to modern hives, inferior however to the People's Hive with fixed combs, but convenient for commercial use.

Since then, we have searched for and ultimately found very simple cages which allow extraction of honey from fixed-comb hives by means of an extractor.

Therefore it is now the People's Hive with fixed combs that deserves everyone's attention, for the People's Hive with fixed combs is an economical hive par excellence: easy to build, in any case less expensive – no frames or foundation; fewer inspections; opening the hive only once a year; 12 kg winter provisions instead of between 15 and 18 kg; respect for the laws of nature, thus no diseases.

Construction of the People's Hive with fixed combs

The People's Hive with fixed combs comprises a floor, three identical boxes and a roof.

The floor is the same size as the exterior of the hive-body boxes and is between 15 and 20 mm thick. The entrance to the hive is made through the depth of the floor.

This entrance through the depth of the floor is 120 mm wide and 40 mm deep if the walls of the hive-body box are 20 mm thick. The resulting notch in the floor is closed with a piece of wood 160 mm square (alighting board).

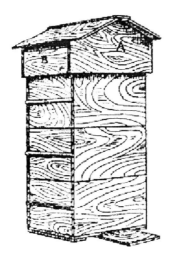

The alighting board is nailed underneath the floor in such a way that a piece 70 x 160 mm projects to the front. One could make the alighting board 410 mm long to strengthen the floor.

The boxes rest directly on the floor and one above the other without interlocking.

There should be at least three boxes. Two boxes contain the brood nest in winter and spring. The third is added only for the nectar flow. But all three boxes are the same size. The inside dimensions of them are 210 mm deep and 300 mm wide (length and breadth).

At the top of the inside rim of the boxes, on two opposite sides, there is a need to make rebates to hold the combs (top-bars). These rebates are 10 mm wide and 10 mm deep. The thickness of the walls of the boxes should be at least 20 mm.

On two exterior surfaces of each box are placed handles to ease manipulation.

Each box should contain eight top-bars (comb supports). These top-bars have the following dimensions: 9 x 24 x 315 mm.

The top-bars are fixed in the rebates with small pins, for example glaziers' pins. Moreover, these top-bars are placed at a distance of 36 mm between centres. Between each of them there is therefore a gap of 12 mm for the bees to pass. There is also a gap of 12 mm between the end bars and the adjacent walls of the box. This space allows the entire comb construction.

The roof surrounds the top box with a play of 10 mm. The roof contains a sheet of material which covers the top-bars, and a quilt.

The quilt has the same length and breadth as the outside of the boxes. It should be 100 mm deep. Underneath the quilt is a sheet of coarse cloth. The square part of the roof will have the same depth plus 20 mm. This square part is covered with boards which at the same time serve as covers for the quilt.

The angled part of the roof is empty and open on four faces. There is free passage of air at the top of the gables A (see p. 44, shaded area) and at the top of the eaves B (shaded area).

We have said that the roof contains a sheet of material that covers the top-bars of the top box to stop the bees sticking the top-bars to the quilt.

This sheet of material may be cut from used sacking. Its size should be at least 360 x 360 mm to begin with.

To prevent the bees from fraying this sheet of material, it is moistened with flour paste.

To give this sheet of material the necessary shape and size it is placed still wet on the box. When it is dry, it is trimmed following the outer edges of the box. If the final cut of the material is made before wetting it, it will subsequently no longer be possible to obtain the necessary size.

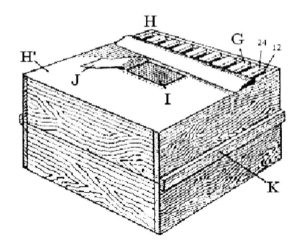

Hive-body box of the People's Hive: G – eight top-bars rest in rebates at each end. They are 24 mm wide and separated by a gap of 12 mm. H' – a coarse cloth covering the top box at all times; I – a metal mesh filling a slot in H; J – another piece of coarse cloth covering I. This fitting allows feeding with an upturned jam-jar. We prefer to use our large feeder. K – handle to facilitate manipulation. It is preferable to align it with the direction of the top-bars. Avoid replacing this handle with a notch in the box or a metal handle as manipulation would then be more difficult.

Flour paste

In order to make the flour paste, mix into a litre of water four or five soup-spoonfuls of wheat flour, or better still, rye flour. Boil it while stirring with a spoon until it becomes a thick, homogenous paste. It is good to add a small amount of starch to the flour.

Economy roof for the People's Hive

The sloping roof is more stylish. The one described here is cheaper and suffices. However, it is better to give the side pieces a width of 160 mm instead of 40 mm to enable them fully to cover the quilt which is 100 mm deep and to enclose the top box to a depth of 20 mm.

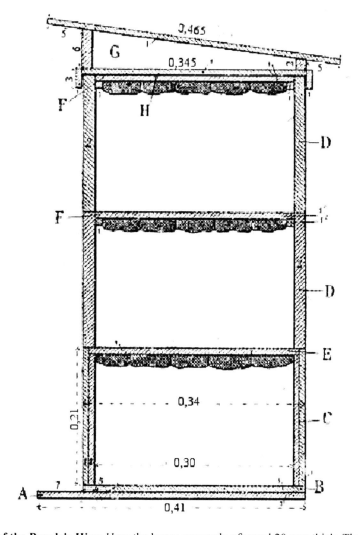

Cross-section of the People's Hive: Here the boxes are made of wood 20 mm thick. The lower box C is made of two sheets of 10 mm thick wood superimposed as can be found in old packing-cases. This is illustrated to show what can be done to economise. Other thicknesses can be used, but it is important to retain the internal dimensions of each box as 300 x 300 x 210 mm. F – the top-bars rest on battens. They are easier to make than a rebate, but they make it more difficult to remove the combs. E – the top-bars rest on one thickness of wood that forms the rebate. The starter-strips hang under the top-bars. Here the hive is covered with a cheaper style of roof. There is no quilt below it.

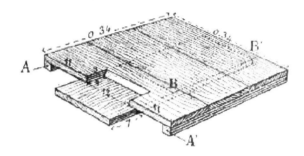

Floor of the People's Hive: The sizes given are for a hive whose boxes have walls 20 mm thick. The battens at A and A' do not have any fixed width if not being used with our cast iron legs. In the latter case they would have to be at least 60 mm wide.

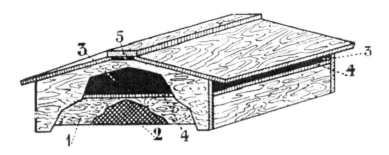

Sloping roof of the People's Hive:

1 – Wooden quilt 100 mm tall.
2 – Coarse cloth fixed underneath the quilt to support the insulating material: chopped oat straw, sawdust, etc.
3 & 5 – Cavity permitting a continuous flow of air.
4 – isolating board that prevents access of mice to the quilt. It is fixed to the roof.
5 – gap formed by assembly of the wood.

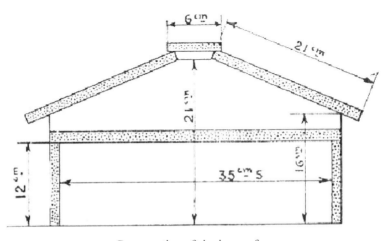

Cross section of sloping roof

44

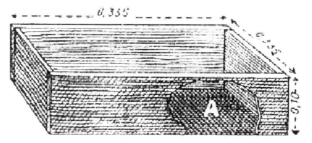

Quilt: A – pack-cloth or old sacking.

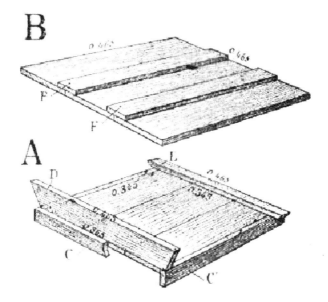

Economical sloping roof for The People's Hive: B – top; A – base.

Observation

The basic rule in the People's Hive is to give each box internal dimensions as follows: depth: 210 mm; width and breadth 300 mm with a rebate of 10 x 10 mm.

The external dimensions may vary according to the thickness of the wood used.

The floor must have a maximum size the same as the external dimensions of a box. It is preferable to make it a millimetre less on all sides so that it will not trap water.

The quilt must have an exterior the same length and breadth as a box, less 5 mm to facilitate working. The roof should enclose the quilt and cover the top box by 20 mm with a play of 10 mm to facilitate removal and replacement.

Discussion of the People's Hive

Ábbé Émile Warré

Legs

There is cause to examine the height and shape of the hive legs. Both are important.

Firstly the height: beekeepers often make their hive stands tall. Everyone likes to feel comfortable. They do not want to bend down. But I estimate that the colonies need only be opened rarely, much less often than in general.

As a result, it is a much smaller sacrifice that I ask of my readers, and not without good reason, when I advise them to place their hives 100 or 150 mm from the ground.

Placed on raised stands, the hives are subject to variations in temperature and to gusts of wind.

Moreover, buying or making such stands amounts to a significant expense. I have seen such stands made from a framework whose wood would have been sufficient to make a double-walled hive.

I know very well that one can save money by using two light wooden beams or metal girders. These would be supported in between by some light brickwork; furthermore they would run the full length of the hive. Colonies may be placed at 750 mm between centres. Unfortunately, this arrangement is inconvenient in covered apiaries. As soon as one colony is touched the rest take notice and begin to hum. There is thus at each hive opening an untimely consumption of honey. Sometimes it triggers robbing and makes the bees angry.

Raising the hives too high also causes a large loss of foragers. It is not unusual that these brave workers return too heavily laden, miss the entrance of the hive and fall on the ground. They climb only with difficulty into a raised hive.

Hive leg in cast iron

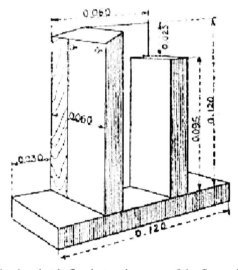

Wooden hive leg that is fixed at each corner of the floor with four nails

One can of course place a wide board coming from the ground to the entrance of the hive. It is an additional expense which still does not prevent the bees from falling at the sides.

We can equally say that raising the hive protects the hive and its colony from moisture from the ground and its vegetation. But I hold that there should never be vegetation surrounding hives. Ground vegetation is the bane of bees. When a bee falls into it loaded with its forage, it finds darkness, coolness, and soon the cold, but nothing to warm it up and invigorate it. On bare ground, however, the bee can receive the rays of the sun until the last. It will often have time to rest sufficiently to be able to get back into its hive.

But the wetness of the ground! A hive placed 100 mm from the ground is perfectly protected from this wetness, if the vegetation is removed, and if the hive contains no other opening for ventilation underneath.

Obviously, the short legs make it easier for the re-entry of the bees surrounding the hive who have lost their way.

It is therefore sufficient and preferable not to make the stands taller than 100 mm.

But what shape should these stands have? Do not consider using beams to support several hives at once. We have given reasons for this in the preceding. Cast iron legs are commercially available. With these, the hive floors are well isolated from the ground, but such feet have the fault that they also require one to use a tile, otherwise they would sink into the ground.

We have perfected a hive leg that ends in the shape of a duck's foot and cannot sink into the ground. It simplifies manipulation and strengthens the base of the hive.

We have also designed a wooden leg with the same characteristics, apart from its strength, as the cast iron one. Moreover, it is more economical and can be made without any special tools from wood off-cuts.

These legs can be replaced by a hollow brick.

This kind of brick, which is 110 mm on its four faces, isolates the floor from the ground satisfactorily and costs less. The hollow brick could be replaced by two ordinary bricks placed flat, on top of each other. But these bricks allow a certain amount of dampness to rise and increase the amount of work needed. Moreover they need repositioning from time to time. Clearly, bricks do not make the job easier as much as do our steel legs.

The floor

The floor is for closing the hive at the bottom, whilst at the same time allowing access for both the bees and fresh air.

What wood should be used for the floor? The thicker the wood the longer it will last. However, if the wood is very thick it will be heavy to handle; if it is too thin it will not resist bad weather or the knocks it will receive for long.

A thickness of between 15 mm and 20 mm is a good and sufficient thickness, all the more so for it being reinforced by battens underneath.

What should the bees' entrance be like? People have given it a length of the full width of the hive and a height of between 10 mm and 20 mm. I am of the opinion that such a length, which goes beyond 400 mm in certain hives, is definitely harmful. During the course of the summer the population may diminish and not be able to defend itself on such a front. The supporters of big entrances say that they reduce them when necessary. But they may forget such surveillance. In any case, it is extra work that we do not want. It is not without reason that we have given the entrance to the People's Hive the following size: 120 x 15 mm. But we draw attention to the fact that we prefer that size to 200 x 10 mm which gives the same access mathematically speaking. With an entrance of 120 x 15 mm, the bees have less distance to cover; a weak colony will thus defend itself more easily.

Of course, in winter, we reduce this entrance further. A metal entrance has an opening of only 70 x 7.5 mm to prevent the entry of rodents. Moreover, in winter there are not that many bee sorties. This opening serves, so to speak, only for ventilating the hive.

Furthermore, the entrance of 120 x 15 mm is enough to allow passage of the bees even of a strong colony. To confirm this, it is sufficient to watch their comings and goings during full nectar flow. The opening is also sufficient for ventilating the hive: passage of fresh air to replace the lighter air leaving at the top. Do not forget that a hive even in summer contains only 30 to 35 litres of air. To give access to such a volume of air, it is not necessary to have a large opening, all the more so because this volume of air should not be replaced without reason. We will discuss this again under 'Ventilation'.

Why then put mesh covered openings in the floor, leaving some openings opposite the entrance above the floor? All these openings complicate construction of the hive and increase its capital cost. They are useless, because the entrance I have described above is sufficient for ventilating the hive. Furthermore, they are harmful.

An opening opposite the entrance above the floor makes defending the colony difficult. It might also create an air current which, in winter, would detach bees from the cluster and they would come to a certain death on the floor.

An opening on the floor is always a collecting place for wax and bee debris, a sure hiding place for insects, above all wax moth. Such an opening allows dampness from the ground to rise more easily into the hive.

When the various hive systems are studied, it can be seen that the floor is always fixed to the hive body by very different methods.

These floors are always difficult to clean, even in hives said to be automatic.

For our People's Hive, we prefer the floor whose description we have already given.

The hive body comprises two easily manoeuvrable boxes. Without uncovering these boxes one can lift them, place them on stands and then deal freely with the floor, clean it, check if it is level, clear the ground underneath it.

The two boxes are then replaced on the floor. There is no danger of crushing bees nor of chilling the brood.

Brood chamber

The brood chamber in a hive is the part that contains the colony and the winter stores. Here, the brood chamber comprises two boxes.

It is important to consider in principle the volume of the brood chamber, for its volume should be as small as possible in order to reduce the consumption of stores, as the bee eats not only to nourish itself but also to warm itself. Brood chambers vary from 36 litres, as with the People's Hive, to 55 litres, as with the Dadant hive.

All evidence shows that bees consume more in a large brood chamber than in a small one. I even venture to say that the difference is between 3 kg and 5 kg. And this is each year. For the beekeeper this is a loss that quickly doubles the price of his hive.

A large hive also has the inconvenience of keeping bees in on the first fine days, a time when they would be able to find a lot of pollen and a little nectar outside. Big hives thus do not make strong colonies; they act on the fecundity of queens only by delaying its manifestation.

Partitions (follower/division boards) can of course be placed in big hives to vary their size. But these partitions are inconvenient for several reasons.

In autumn, they impede the free distribution of winter stores. If they do not fit close to the walls, they are useless; if they do fit close they are stuck with propolis and require a sharp bang each time you want to move them. Now bees meet violence with violence. Furthermore, all moving of partitions uses up the beekeeper's time and cools the brood chamber, a further cause of dissatisfaction amongst the bees.

The volume of the brood chamber should nevertheless be adequate. It should allow accommodation of honey for winter stores, of the bees under the honey, and the laying by the queen in spring.

But it should be noted that in winter and at the beginning of spring the needs of the bees are appreciably similar in all hives, because the colonies differ little in strength. The diameter of the cluster of bees hardly varies more than one or two centimetres from one hive to another.

And Abbé Voirnot, who studied this issue the most, concluded that 100 square decimetres of comb suffice in winter and early spring.

Dr. Duvauchelle, our first beekeeping mentor, was convinced that small hives are better, having created a hive of 280 x 360 mm, therefore 80 square decimetres of comb. Later he enlarged his hive and gave it 9 frames of 300 x 400 mm with 96 square decimetres of comb. This showed his approval of Abbé Voirnot's conclusions. We too have confirmed that these two masters were right on this point.

Combs

The combs may be moveable or fixed. They are referred to as moveable when they are enclosed in a wooden frame, as in modern hives. But we should note well that they only really remain moveable on condition that they are cleaned every year.

Combs are described as fixed when they are not surrounded by wood and because the bees fix them to the walls of the hive boxes. But because they are fixed with wax they are in fact more moveable than moveable combs fixed with propolis.

We have preferred the fixed comb for several reasons. Firstly, frames are expensive, and, as we have already said, often useless. In addition, frames increase the volume of the brood nest. Earlier, we presented two People's Hives, one with and one without fixed combs. They both had the same number of square decimetres of comb. But the framed hive had a volume of 44 litres, whereas that of the fixed-comb hive was 36 litres, because the frames increase hive size. And we said previously that big brood chambers harm bees and beekeepers. In framed hives, we had a winter consumption 3 kg more than in fixed hives.

The combs can vary in shape. They can be shallow as in the Dadant, or deep, as in the Layens, or square, as in the Voirnot.

In many skeps, where bees have lived for centuries, we frequently find a width of 300 mm and a depth varying between 600 mm and 800 mm. The Layens frame and the deep Congrès frame gave us good results. They had widths of 310 mm and 300 mm. Furthermore, a width of 300 mm allows a square brood chamber to be set up. And the square shape, after that of the cylinder, contributes well to distributing the warmth in the hive. This width also permits us to give the hive an elongated shape (vertically) like a cluster of bees; it equally enables the bees to put their honey at the top of the hive, install themselves underneath the honey, and allows them to insert the head of their cluster in the stock of honey, just as our head is inserted into our hat. This is the best arrangement for wintering.

In the winter cluster of bees, there is really only life at the top and at the centre, because only there is there sufficient warmth. Around the edges of the cluster, the bees are torpid, half dead.

All the bees, it is true, pass in their turn to the centre of the cluster to warm themselves and to feed. But they do not have sufficient strength to leave the cluster. It is this that explains how bees on long, shallow frames can die of hunger beside an abundance of stores. During cold periods, they cannot easily move horizontally, whether from frame to frame or on the same frame. But, on the other hand, they move easily vertically, from bottom to top, as movement takes them towards the warmth which is always greater at the top of the hive.

Abbé Voirnot thought he had failed to improve the Dadant frame. But he stopped at a square frame of 330 mm because he attached considerable importance to the cubic shape of the brood nest.

The cubic shape of the hive outside may be taken into consideration, because it reduces the surface of the hive and as a result the heat dissipation.

But the dissipation is minimal in the interior of the hive. In the brood chamber, what is important to consider above all, is the heat that is enclosed. Now this heat presents itself there as layers one on top of the other, all the warmer for being deeper. And these layers of heat are deeper the less wide they are, thus they re-warm the bees all the better if the combs are not so wide.

The deep frame is superior not only in winter but also in spring. When a colony extends its brood nest by one centimetre, it must heat this centimetre over all its surface. It will have to heat 2,000 cubic centimetres in the Dadant hive but only 900 cubic centimetres in the People's Hive. This is why I adopted a width of comb of 300 mm and two depths of 200 mm. These two depths one above the other have all the advantages of a single depth of 400 mm. This arrangement gives a space of 13 mm between the boxes. These 13 mm comprise the 9 mm of the top-bars and the 4 mm gap left by the bees at the bottoms of the combs, being the thickness of the bee body, for the bee, when working with its underside in the air, cannot extend the comb where its body is.

This gap suits the bees in winter as it facilitates communication within the cluster of bees. If the gap did not exist, the bees themselves would create holes across the combs as they do in the frames of other hives.

However, I consider the gap a fault, because the bees have to heat it almost wastefully in spring. It is a single fault, and moreover small beside the advantages that result from this arrangement, an even smaller fault than that of modern hives where the bees have uselessly to heat very much greater voids.

However, to avoid difficulties for the beekeeper at the moment of putting the winter stores in order as well as avoiding increasing for the bees the number of these gaps in the middle of the brood chamber, I adopted combs of 200 mm, and not shallower ones, as is generally done for hives with tiered body-boxes (supers, ekes), referred to as divisible hives.

If the deep frame is greatly advantageous in winter, just as in early spring, it may have its inconveniences in summer. If there is a residue of stores, when there have been some small amounts of nectar coming in, there may be a band of honey at the top of the frame. But bees greatly dislike crossing over honey. They rise with difficulty into the super and often prefer to swarm. This is why bees go up into supers sooner in hives with shallow frames.

In the People's Hive, we have the advantages of a deep frame without its disadvantages, because enlargement is made at the bottom.

Hive body

If a small brood nest is adequate for bees in winter and early spring, in summer they want a bigger hive comprising the brood nest and an additional box, or several of them. With the People's Hive we regard this supplementary box as a minimum. We have had colonies occupying seven boxes.

The number of boxes necessary varies with the wealth of nectar production in the region and with the fecundity of each queen. It is therefore wise to have at one's disposal several supplementary boxes, especially in small apiaries. In large apiaries there are always some unoccupied hives whose boxes are available.

The People's Hive is thus a small hive in winter, but in summer it can be as big as the biggest of hives.

It should be noted that the boxes are placed on top of each other without any interlocking. They can be fixed to the floor and to each other by some article of ironmongery or simply by two nails linked by plain steel wire, and this on two or three surfaces. Barring movement of the hives, these measures are of no use. The weight of the boxes does not allow the wind to move them. Furthermore, the bees join them with their propolis.

The walls

The most healthy walls are those of the old skeps, in straw or osier, covered with daub. These walls are warm in winter, cool in summer and permeable at all times. They do not keep the humidity in. They attenuate variations in temperature. In practice, because we need the regularity of a square form, we give preference to wood. Wood requires less monitoring and maintenance. As insects often hide in the straw, rodents attack more readily.

Wood is more resistant to insects, rodents and bad weather. A coat of white oil-based paint can, moreover, be quickly given, without driving the bees out.

We thus settle for wooden walls of 24 mm thick.

A thickness of 20 mm is sufficient. A thickness 24 mm is preferable only from the point of view of strength. There is less play in the wood at this thickness. Furthermore, in such hives, the bees go out sooner in the mornings because they sense more readily the ambient temperature.

Thicker walls increase the weight of the hive and its capital cost.

Double walls have the same disadvantage. In addition it is almost impossible to retain the enclosed air that should be an insulator and thus useful.

The insulating materials that can be placed between two boards are often expensive; they sometimes absorb moisture and cease to be insulators.

Furthermore, the insulating walls do not achieve their aim. In spring they delay the bees foraging sorties. In winter they do not economise on stores. On the contrary, the bees consume less when they are torpid with cold than when they are kept active.

Certainly in snowy weather, a ray of sunshine makes a few bees go out from hives with thin walls, more than from those with thick walls. Some settle on the snow or on the alighting board and die there. The cluster of several thousand bees is not noticeably reduced. Moreover, those bees that do not come back in again are probably weak, old, of no value.

Certainly, if single-walled hives are more susceptible to the ambient temperature by day, they are equally susceptible to the cold at night. But at night, the presence of the bees compensates for the lack of warmth.

And let us not forget that comfort weakens the stock, that striving, as Pourrat said, is the condition of life, adversity its climate.

Theoretically white wood is preferable. Unfortunately there is too much play in it. In practice we prefer Jura pine (*Abies alba*).

Some prefer half-jointed construction. We prefer butt-jointed construction. It is a lot more economical and does not require professional tools. If 60–70 mm nails are used and wood that is somewhat seasoned, it will be satisfactory.

In any case, we prefer wood planed on two surfaces, thus straight, to have the straightness both on the exterior and the interior. Otherwise rain collects on projecting parts and cleaning the inside will be more difficult.

The roof

The roof of the People's Hive is arranged in a way such that it contains a large void at its top. The air circulates rapidly and freely in this void. Furthermore, the void is too big for cobwebs to be able to stop the circulation of air there.

It is under this type of roof that I have observed a more regular temperature, even when the hive is exposed to the sun.

At the battle-front, I had the occasion to see some light military buildings. The roof was also formed from two planks or from two overlapping sheets of metal. A high-ranking officer who had lived long in the colonies told me that military tents were designed on the same principle to combat the heat of the sun.

The design of our roof is thus well established according to rules dictated by experience.

Roofs are often covered by bituminous felt. I am not in favour of this. It is an expense. Furthermore, bituminous felt often traps moisture out of sight which rots the board that supports it.

I am not in favour of sheet metal. In rainy weather or hail it produces a sound sufficient to disturb the bees. Moreover, it is permeable to the heat of the sun.

I prefer painted wood. A board painted every two or three years lasts a long time and does not have the faults of bituminous felt or sheet metal. But additionally, I prefer white paint that reflects heat. Creosote, which is undoubtedly the best wood preserver, is not suitable because of its smell and above all because of its colour.

Cloth

On top of the top box we place a simple coarse cloth, that we often get from pieces of old sacks.

We prefer this cloth to oilcloth and to boards. Boards are impermeable and require force, a shock, when one wants to lift them. The bees get angry.

Oilcloth is impermeable and does not peel off as easily as plain cloth.

For, let us not forget, everything we put on the hive is propolised and as a result sticks to it. We may therefore only look for an easy way of removing it.

Yet our cloth peels off easily. We take it by one left corner and pull it horizontally to the right. In this operation, there is no shock and we only uncover the part we want access to.

Furthermore, the main quality of this cloth is its permeability that the bees can modify, augment or reduce, adding to or removing from the cloth the propolis that they deposit everywhere. This propolis allows the bees themselves to ventilate the People's Hive as they did in the old skeps. It is good to renew this cloth frequently. Furthermore, pieces of it can be put to use in the roll of paper for the smoker.

Quilt

The quilt is 100 mm deep and not 50 mm, as with conventional ones. The underneath is covered by a cloth. But the top is open. It is filled with sawdust, chopped straw, peat, or any other light material that is absorbent and poorly conducts heat.

The quilt is not closed, so its contents can easily be renewed.; in any case stir it often to keep it dry, because it absorbs the hive's moisture more easily and conducts less of the outside heat to the hive. When one has sawdust or chopped straw at one's disposal it can be renewed annually. If the old insulation is spread around the hive it suppresses weed growth.

Ventilation

Moisture is generated in any hive by the life of the animals and by the evaporation of nectar. There is also stale air resulting from animal respiration.

This stale, humid air is warm when it is in the cluster of bees and thus it tends to rise. Reaching the top of the hive, it does not cool down quickly, because the top of the hive is always warm, and because the walls of the People's Hive are never very cold, due to the shorter distance between them and the bee cluster. This stale air will then continue to occupy the top of the hive, but the cloth lets it pass and be taken into the quilt.

This escape of stale air draws in fresh air through the hive entrance. As this escape of air is continuous and under the control of the bees, the fresh air enters only slowly but continuously, to renew the air in the hive and without making the bees uncomfortable.

In other hives this ventilation does not take place in the same manner. The stale air is quickly stopped by the oilcloth or crown boards and continues to surround the bees, for in hives bigger than the People's Hive, the bees are closer to the top.

This stale air extends as far as the walls and condenses on contact with them as they are further away from the bee cluster and thus cooler than the walls of the People's Hive.

Having condensed, the moist air passes down the walls and the outer combs and produces moisture and mould.

However big the entrance may be, the fresh air does not enter the hive because it is not drawn in by the departure of the stale air. Ventilation in such hives is insufficient or absent.

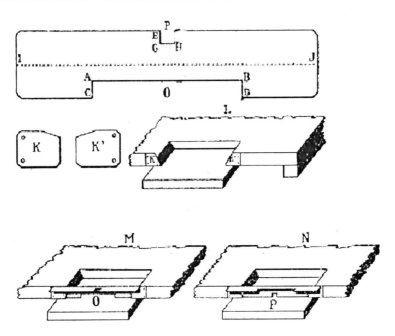

Detail of the entrance: P – 6 x 6 mm hole. O – 70 x 7.5 mm hole.

For some time I have seen people advising the cutting of an opening of several centimetres in crown boards covering the hive. This is certainly a radical means of avoiding mouldy frames and walls; but one wonders how beekeepers dare to give such advice. This opening is too big for the bees to be able to close it. Furthermore, people are advised to prevent them doing so. The bees can no longer control the escape of air through this opening. There is thus a continuous current of air through it right through the winter season. This can only be at the expense of the bees and their stores.

Entrance

Our entrance is one of great simplicity. It can be cut out of an empty food can. The entrance to the hive can be readily reduced without squashing bees and gives them, as required, an entrance of 70 x 7.5 mm to prevent the entrance of mice and shrews, or of 6 x 6 mm allowing passage of only one bee at a time to feed or when there is a risk of robbing.

Top-bars

The top-bar (comb support) has a width of 24 mm. We prefer to give it a thickness of only 9 mm so that it never projects out of the 10 mm rebate of the box.

Furthermore, it is preferable that the top-bars are not planed on the lower surface; this is to facilitate adherence of the wax. On the other hand, it is preferable that the three other surfaces are planed in order to make it easier to clean them. The propolisation of these three surfaces could even be reduced by coating them with Vaseline or oil.

Initial conclusions

Beekeeping is an industry

Beekeeping can be profitable. This profit should be the aim of the beekeeper.

And just as no beekeeper says that for him beekeeping is only a hobby, none do it only for its profits. We have brothers, do not forget, unfortunate brothers who have no experience of beneficent work. Give to them what nature gives to you in excess.

But how can we get the maximum profits from beekeeping?

Let us not rely on import restrictions

Relying on import restrictions is often an illusion, because political parties are opposed to it. In any case, such protectionism is often a mistake, because it increases the sale price and that makes selling the product more difficult.

Let us look at the economy

Industrialists have the principle: produce cheaply to sell easily.

Beekeepers should adopt this principle. They will avoid at the same time the annoyance of the sale of honey at a loss and they will come to gain from beekeeping the highest possible profit.

It is not impossible that in the future the sale price of honey will be fixed around the price of sugar, which would, moreover, make its sale a lot easier. It is therefore important to try to produce it for as little as possible.

Now, what we have said about the construction of the People's Hive is sufficient to show its advantages from the point of view of economics.

We will see later that the method applied to it is as economical as its construction.

Economy through its design

It is clear that the People's Hive is sufficiently simplified for any amateur to be able to make it with an ordinary set of tools. Our indications generally suffice. In any case, only one pattern will be necessary.

It is not the same as a framed hive. The frame alone is time consuming and requires care. Frame bars have to be very straight. There has to be a gap of 7.5 mm between the frame uprights and the inside walls of the hive. When there is less than 5 mm, the bees stick the uprights and walls together with propolis. When there is more than 10 mm, the bees construct comb in the gap. In either case there is no longer any mobility. As usage and temperature cause variations in one direction or the other, it is necessary that at manufacture there is a gap of exactly 7.5 mm between the frames and the walls. This is difficult to achieve and maintain.

Economy through its size

The shape and the volume of the People's Hive guarantees the minimum consumption of honey whilst at the same time allowing the bees to develop normally.

Economy through its hygienic properties

The shape, the volume and the ventilation of the People's Hive give the bees a healthy home where they are saved from over exertion, weakening and disease, all things which necessarily reduce the production of honey.

Equipment

Smoker

The smoker is the most essential piece of equipment for anyone wanting to get involved with bees. There are many different types. Each person may choose according to both what they prefer and the fuel they have available.

However, the most popular smokers are the Layens and the Bingham.

The Layens smoker has the advantage of giving a gentle steady flow of smoke, and of burning unattended for a quarter of an hour. It works by clockwork. This smoker also has its disadvantages. Its fire-box is not big enough so it has to be fed often. It will not give a strong smoke flow when it may be required. Furthermore, its clockwork makes a noise that does not please the bees of the colony being opened, still less those in the next colony. Finally, the clockwork is rather fragile which makes the Layens smoker very expensive.

In my opinion, the Bingham smoker is the most practical, above all the small model. It fits well in the hand. It gives a gentle flow of smoke when required, and a dense and abundant one. When not in use and stood with its nozzle in the air, it does not, like the Layens, annoy the bees, and it only uses up a small amount of fuel without, however, going out.

In this smoker use rolls of corrugated paper or cheap cloth (from wrappings, old sacks). These rolls must have a diameter a little less than that of the smoker, so they can be inserted easily. Their length should be two-thirds of the length of the inside of the smoker, so a new one can be inserted when the remainder of the preceding one is still there. In this way, it is lit once, there is no lack of smoke and the smoke never contains sparks.

From time to time, before inserting a new roll, the old one is removed from the smoker and the cinders that have accumulated at the bottom are tipped out. The partly burnt roll is reinserted and supplemented with a new one.

In dry weather the rolls burn too quickly. They can be moistened a little. They then burn more slowly and give more smoke. Of course, one must put the dry part in first.

When the top-bar cover-cloth impregnated with propolis is renewed, it is a good idea to put a piece of it in the smoker roll. One can also put in small pieces of propolis.

Brush

A brush is useful to the beekeeper. It helps, with the smoker, to guide the bees, in any case to remove the last bees from the combs to be taken.

Where possible, this brush should be of traditional design and of the very best quality, entirely of natural silk. Otherwise it catches on the bees and annoys them. The brush should be kept very clean and never be used when wet to avoid it sticking to the bees.

Veil

A veil is not absolutely necessary. Many beekeepers do not use them, even for difficult operations.

All beekeepers, however, ought to possess at least two veils, one for themselves and one for a helper. And these veils should always be to hand during all work on hives. If there is an accident, these veils will be useful.

Most beekeepers, especially beginners, wear a veil for all beekeeping work.

By means of the veil they will feel safer and more confident, so they will work faster and with greater skill.

But there are lots of different veils which do not all have the same usefulness. Let us consider the two main ones: the fabric net veil and the metal one.

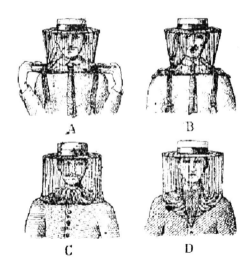

Fabric net veils

The fabric net veil has the advantage that it does not take up any room and it can be put in the pocket. But it has the disadvantage of making the operator's head feel hotter and impairs his vision.

Black veils increase heat the most, and impair vision the least. White veils cause least increase in heat and most impairment of vision.

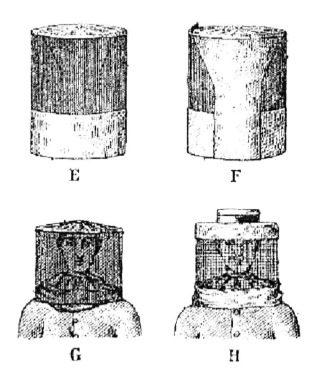

Veils made of metal mesh

Black net can be put at the front and white at the back. In any case, one can always choose a net of a larger mesh size without, however, going beyond 3 mm.

Veil size varies according to its support, usually a hat, and according to the head of the wearer.

At the top it is closed with an elastic band which encompasses the hat. At the bottom it is also closed with an elastic band which encompasses an upright collar or is fixed with a button (D); or it may be free and tucked under the braces (A and B), or it is tucked under the topmost garment (C). The top of the veil can also be attached to the rim of the hat. In this case it cannot be carried in the pocket. It then has the disadvantages of the metallic veil without any of its advantages.

The metallic veil is less portable than the fabric net one, in the other hand it is less inclined to make one hot or impair vision. To make it, the metal mesh that is used for making food safes is suitable. Galvanised mesh impairs vision. Black mesh is preferable. Black metal mesh that is covered in varnish is available. This is the best.

The height and diameter of the veil are in proportion to the head of the beekeeper. The veil should leave a gap of 50 mm around the head. The top of the metal veil is closed with a pleated cloth (E, F). There is no need for a hat with this veil. The metal veil is extended at the bottom with cloth that can likewise be tucked under the braces (A, B), or under the topmost garment (G) or as in C. At the back of the veil is placed a strip of cloth to provide shade and also to cover the ends of the wires of the metal mesh (F). To make it stiffer all round, it is a good idea to attach a thin piece of steel wire to the top and to the bottom of the metal mesh while one is attaching the cloths.

Finally, a combination veil can be made (H) .

The picture shows how it is made. A strip of cloth is attached to the rim of a hat, the strip of metal mesh is added, then another strip of cloth.

As with the other veils, the second strip of cloth can be tucked under the braces (A, B), or under the topmost garment (G). This veil requires the wearing of a hat and makes one hotter than a veil entirely of metal mesh. On the other hand, it is more secure on the head.

Stands

In various beekeeping tasks to be done with the People's Hive, there is often a need for one or two stands to put the boxes on. The stands illustrated in the figure B fulfil this purpose perfectly.

B: Batten stands for boxes (hive bodies)

Note that the battens A'A' are ridged at the top so as to avoid crushing bees. They also need to be 100 mm longer than the boxes so as to make it easy to place the box on them. The battens B'B are simply to link and fix the ridged battens. A'A'.

Hive tool

This hive tool is made specially for cleaning the tops of the top-bars which are always coated with propolis.

Hive tool

The hive tool is also for separating the boxes and lifting them. The curved part can be used to lift the top-bars when the honey is harvested.

Toolbox

Beekeepers at work need a number of small objects that would be difficult, not to say annoying, to have to carry in the hands. Furthermore, it is necessary to cover the scrapings and comb debris in order to avoid robbing.

This is why boxes are made, called toolboxes, of different shapes according to the preferences and needs of each beekeeper.

The main thing is to have two compartments, one for tools and the other for comb debris and hive tools, the latter compartment covered in order to avoid triggering robbing.

Special feeder

We have indicated elsewhere several ways of feeding the bees. Here we speak of our special feeder, as it can be of great service to beekeepers, above all when getting the hives ready for winter.

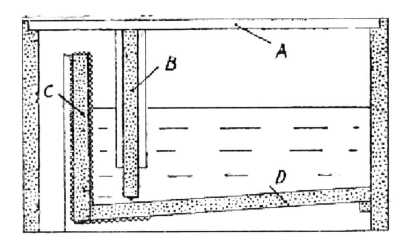

Autumn feeder

This feeder is made of painted wood which makes it superior to metal feeders. With metal feeders, if there is a leak, it is serious and could drown the bees. Repair can only be done by a specialist. With the wooden feeder, there is never more than a seepage. A layer of paint when it is dry is all that is needed to make it disappear. This feeder is the same size as a hive-body box and has a volume of 11 litres. It is rare that a colony needs a supplement so great. One night thus often suffices to complete the stores of one colony. For, it is important to feed rapidly. In any case, a sheet of glass is put over the feeder and allows one to see what is happening. Its design also means it can be filled without smoker or veil.

Inside is a vertical, moveable board held by two nails at its base, allowing the syrup to pass into the compartment where the bees come to feed, without letting them drown in the syrup.

If comb debris is used instead of syrup this board is removed.

This feeder is placed above the brood chamber and not below it. On the feeder is placed the cloth that covers the top-bars, the quilt and then the roof. One feeder is enough for 12 hives.

This feeder is housed in a hive-body box of the People's Hive. (see p. 60)

A. Board of 50 mm wide with a hole in it allowing refilling the feeder with a funnel. It rests in the rebates and on the board B without allowing the bees to pass into the trough. A sheet of glass is positioned to one side of this board completely covering the feeder.

B. Moveable board between battens resting on the bottom with two round-headed 2 mm wide nails allowing the passage of liquid but not the bees. This board is removed when giving comb debris instead of syrup.

C. Fixed board held by a batten and covered with metal mesh leaving a 20 mm wide clearance at the top.

D. Fixed board, resting on battens.

Advice

Put some good quality paint in all the joints during assembly. Give all parts two or three coats of paint. This feeder is placed above the hive body, under the cloth that covers the top-bars and the quilt.

Spring and summer feeder

To feed colonies that are short of stores in spring and summer, and to stimulate comb building in weak colonies, we have another feeder. It will hold 200 g syrup.

Advice

Same advice regarding construction as for the large feeder. The small feeder is placed on the floor under the hive-bodies, its moveable part at the back of the hive.

Uncapping knife

Before putting combs in the extractor it is necessary to remove the cappings which close the cells whose honey is ripe.

To carry out this work, one can use an ordinary table knife if it is very thin and cuts easily.

However, as combs are sometimes irregular, it is better to use an uncapping knife, a knife with a cranked handle, special for the purpose.

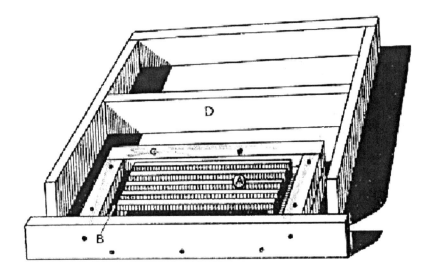

Spring and summer feeder

A. Float made of 9 mm wooden rods side by side.
B. Trough 20 mm deep. External dimensions: length 250 mm; width 150 mm.
C. Frame forming drawer.
D. Frame having the external dimensions of a hive-body box and a height of 2 mm more than the frame in C.

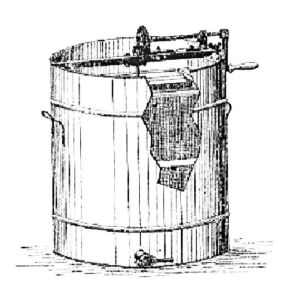

Extractor

Extractor

The extractor is designed to remove honey from the combs with greater speed than by draining under gravity. The combs are placed in wire mesh cages in the middle of a drum which is usually of tinned metal sheeting.

A rotating movement, at the rate of a kilometre in three minutes, brings about a centrifugal force on the comb. The wax is retained by the wire mesh, but the honey goes through the mesh and rains against the sheet metal wall of the tank at the bottom of which it flows out through a special tap.

Without doubt an extractor saves the beekeeper time. That is its main advantage and it is that which all inventors have sought to improve on.

Some people also see in the use of the extractor a means of re-using comb, or of saving work for the bees, and saving honey and wax for the beekeeper. We disagree that this is an advantage as we favour frequent renewal of comb.

Choice of extractor

I do not advise trying to make an extractor with a tank and gearing of some kind. It is better that it is assembled by a professional who is a fairly good engineer and a bit of a beekeeper.

Moreover, commercial extractors are often no better made. The workers who make them do not always know what they are for. Strength is not always where it ought to be. Or here and there are folds that cannot be cleaned out. The first honey to enter them rusts them and contaminates all the honey that subsequently passes through the extractor. It is therefore essential to choose an extractor that is well constructed.

Several years ago someone invented a large number of extractors of different shapes, but always intended for making a good yield.

We have ourselves made a double-sided, horizontal parallel extractor. This extractor, also of high yield, has another advantage. Its parts enable the uncapping of combs without breaking them during different procedures.

Despite its size it goes through the smallest doorways, which is a rare feature.

We are of the opinion that all these extractors, ours like the others, do not meet the needs of beekeepers, but require of them a very considerable investment and encumber them the year round, especially during transport.

Useful extractor

We are of the opinion that our ordinary single-sided extractor would suit all. It is taken to the apiary with two or four cages according to the apiary's size.

A four-cage extractor can extract the honey from a hive-body box of the People's Hive in 12 minutes. It is sufficient for extracting in a single day the honey from 30 hives which is the maximum number one can have at a single location.

This extractor can be placed on packing cases or hive-bodies. It is better to buy the three-legged type.

A cover is also advisable. It helps the movement of the cages and protects the beekeeper from a strong current of air.

However, it should be noted that this extractor is really designed for an apiary of 12 to 15 hives. For a smaller apiary, we advise using another means of extraction.

Cages for uncapping and extraction

These cages are extremely useful. They allow time to be saved during uncapping and extraction. They support the most fragile of comb and allow the uncapping and extraction of comb from fixed-comb hives, and even from the comb fragments from skeps.

These cages are essential for extracting fixed comb with an extractor.

A simple cage suffices. Double cages are always used in pairs.

Having a pair would allow a helper to uncap while the extractor is running.

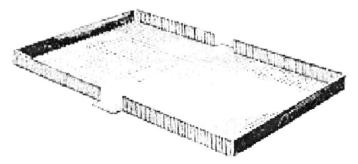

Cage 1 (simple cage): metal sheeting fully tinned, gauge 5/10, size 260 x 365 mm. The sides, 20 mm wide, are bent after cutting the corners. There is no solder. Lugs are inserted on opposite sides by making two cuts in the folded sides.

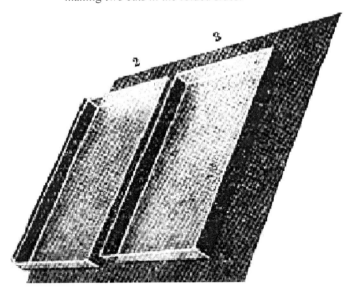

Cage 2: perforated metal sheet, gauge 5/10, size 275 x 380 mm. Holes of 3 mm at 3 mm centres; the sides 20 mm wide are folded after cutting the corners. There is no solder.
Cage 3: perforated tinned metal sheet, gauge 5/10, size 290 x 395 mm. Holes of 3 mm at 3 mm centres; the sides 20 mm are bent after cutting the corners. There is no solder. Cages 2 and 3 constitute the double cage.

Uncapping horse

We present below a picture of it and its method of use (page 116). The horse is only used with the extractor and cages.

Gloves

I must mention gloves, but do so to speak ill of them. Gloves are of no use, even harmful.

They are useless because they do not stop the sting of an angry bee even if made of leather.

They are harmful because they make movement clumsy which always causes crushing of the bees by rough and sudden movements. And all that causes the bees to get angry.

It should even be said that the more gloves appear to guarantee against stings, the more they cause them, because they are more cumbersome.

The helper may puff some smoke from the smoker at the place where the operator is working, accordingly around his hands. They are then completely safe.

The novice beekeeper may, in order to gain steadiness of purpose, ask his helper to puff a little smoke on his hands from time to time. He may then work with more confidence.

Drinker

Bees know how to find the water they need. However, it is not without advantage to put a drinker close to the apiary.

Place on a slightly inclined slab, board or sheet of metal a barrel or jar fitted with a tap. The slab is covered with sand or fine gravel. The tap is adjusted so that it drips and keeps the sand wet.

Amongst beekeeping equipment can be found poultry drinkers which are also suitable for bees.

These comprise a bottle upturned on a metal plate. The plate can be covered with moss, pieces of cork or pebbles.

The apiary

Bees are not very demanding, and no more so regarding the place accorded to them for the hive that shelters them. However, certain comments should be made about the apiary, in the interests of both bee and beekeeper.

Orientation

The bee's greatest enemy is the midday sun. It melts the wax and the honey, destroys combs and drowns bees. Anyway it prevents bees from going out as it forces them to ventilate the hive. It is thus absolutely necessary to shade the hives from the sun with trees: peach, pear, apple, buddleia, etc., or with sunflowers, Jerusalem artichokes, etc.

It is best to face the hives east. The sun rouses the foragers earlier. If this orientation presents difficulties, the hive can if required be pointed west or north, never south.

Size

Hives may take up only 750 mm. The bees recognise their hive perfectly, even in a big apiary, if the hives are placed 750 mm centre to centre.

If the hives are spaced out more than this, the bees are none the worse for it. But the beekeeper has more ground to maintain without any profit.

It does not matter at what angle the bees take wing. However, 45 degrees can be considered a minimum angle. At a lower angle they are inconvenienced.

An example will make this comment clearer. If there is a wall in front of the hives and if it is two metres high, the entrance to the hives should be at least two metres from the wall.

What is given here indicates the size that the apiary should be and the number of hives that will fit on a given piece of land.

Distances

The negligence and imprudence of some beekeepers has resulted in by-laws about distances that should be maintained between hives and public thoroughfares or private land.

These by-laws are for the locality, community or *département*. The scale of this legislation does not allow me to present all of it. It can be found at the headquarters of each *département*.

In general the distances to be maintained vary from between four and six metres. I believe that certain by-laws require a distance of 20 metres. This is exceptional.

It is, however, worth remarking that most of the regulations specify no distance if there is a solid fence etc. two metres tall.

In its sitting of 18 November 1925, the chamber of deputies adopted without debate a proposition drafted thus:

'Single article. – Paragraph 3 of article 17 of the law of 21 June 1898 is amended as follows

'Whereas, hives are not subject to any specification of distance when isolated from neighbouring properties or public thoroughfares by a wall, fence of joined boards, a hedge living or dry without gaps.

'These enclosures should have a height of 2 metres above ground and extend at least 2 metres to each side of the hive.'

Number of hives

The number of hives in a single apiary should be in proportion to the nectar supply in the locality and the number of hives already installed there. Therefore the appropriate number is very variable. It has been estimated, however, that at least 50 hives will prosper within a radius of three kilometres, whatever the wealth of nectar in the area. Of course, the number of neighbouring hives should be taken into account.

Layout

We have already mentioned the difficulties of a covered apiary (opening hives is more difficult) and an open-air apiary on shared stands (the colonies are often agitated, which makes them angry and makes them consume more of their stores). We therefore advise having an open-air apiary with separate stands. This apiary has none of the problems previously mentioned and it is healthier for the beekeeper. They are placed in a single line; or in several parallel lines facing the same way or in opposite directions; or in a horseshoe shape, etc., taking account of what was said in the section 'Orientation'.

Under the hives can be an 800 mm wide concrete paving-stone. If it is considered that the paving-stone dispenses with pulling up weeds round the hives and checking their level in spring, one may find that having this paving-stone is worthwhile, especially if one sets it oneself. A light roof may be put above the hives, or simply grow a Virginia creeper along steel wires.

Planting forage

The beekeeper cannot provide his bees with enough flowers to keep them busy. He needs to rely on the growers in the vicinity.

To be supported by his bees, the beekeeper would have to sow large fields. This would be an additional expense for him and extra effort which would not be paid for in harvested honey.

The beekeeper can plant some ornamental nectar-bearing plants near his hives. He will then sometimes have a chance to follow the work of his bees close at hand. If he has to plant things in his garden or in a neighbouring area of cultivation, he will of course prefer melliferous plants. He may also wish to recommend such plants to his neighbours, and if he wishes follow up his advice with giving them some seeds and a pot of good honey.

The beekeeper should be convinced, and try to convince his neighbours that the more melliferous a plant, the greater its benefit for the farm animals.

The beekeeper will, however, find it worth planting some crocuses, snowdrops, and wallflowers near his apiary. These flowers supply his bees with pollen in early spring when it is as yet in short supply.

Growing lavender can be doubly remunerative.

Growing phacelia could also be considered. It can be sown in spring, at a rate of about 150 to 160 grammes an are (square decametre). It germinates after fourteen days and flowers six weeks later. It reaches a height of 60 centimetres and remains in flower for five weeks. It thus allows successional sowing and provides melliferous flowers when there are none in the area. As it is resistant to the first frosts, it can be sown until 15 August to be green for the livestock at the end of October and the beginning of November.

Beekeeping legislation

Ownership of hives

Article 254 of the civil code: are property by intended purpose when placed by the owner for the service and exploitation of the estate... bee hives.

Ownership of swarms

Article 9 of the law of 4 April 1889: the owner of a swarm has the right to take it, no matter where (even on another's land) so long as he has not stopped following it. Otherwise the swarm belongs to the owner of the land where it settles.

Interference with bees

Article 10 of the law of 4 April 1889: it is not permitted for any reason to disturb bees in their travel or work; as a result, even in cases of legitimate seizure, hives may be moved only in December, January and February.

Accidents

Blunders, mischief by neighbours or passers-by can cause accidents which, before the law, might cost the owner of the bees dear. We recommend that all beekeepers take out accident insurance. Beekeeping associations give a complete guarantee for a minimal premium.

Melliferous plants

On the following page we give a list of melliferous plants which can be cultivated as green or dry forage, or green manure. Lucerne (alfalfa), black medick, phacelia, sainfoin.

In ornamental gardens the following could be planted: aquilegia, angelica, rockcress, borage, honeysuckle, goat's rue, stock, hop, lavender, ivy, sweet marjoram, mallow, snapdragon, catmint, mignonette, rosemary, scabious, thyme, verbena.

In the kitchen garden the following could be left to flower: carrot, brassicae, dandelion.

The following trees are also melliferous: apricot, acacia, olive, cherry, sweet-chestnut, dogwood, maple, ash, holly, horse-chestnut, peach, poplar, pine, pear, apple, plum, fir, willow, *Sorbus*, elder.

Finally, the bees find the following plants growing in the wild: hogweed, briar, selfheal, *Caltha* spp., *Cardamine* (lady's smock), thistle, broom, toad-flax, orchids, bramble, stonecrop, etc.

On the other hand, the following are never allowed near the apiary: tobacco, belladonna, henbane, hemlock, aquilegia, hellebore, rose-laurel, foxglove, thorn-apple, monkshood, varnish-tree, autumn crocus. These plants are not all harmful to bees, but their alkaloids pass into honey which then becomes dangerous.

| Plant name | Soil preference | Time of seeding | Seed amount per hectare (kg) | | Time of harvest (*) | Yield, tonnes per hectare of green forage | |
			random	in rows		from	to
winter rape	calc.-clay, siliceous clay	Aug-Sep	10 - 11,	7 - 8	Feb - end Mar	12	25
spring rape	deep calcareous clay	–	6 - 8,	4	Mar - end Apr	18	30
crimson clover	sandy, calc. -clay	–	25 (de-husked)		Apr - end Jun	18	25
clover hybr. Alsike	–	–	–		–	–	–
winter vetch	clay, calc. -clay	Sep - Oct	180 - 200		May - end Jun	18	50
hairy tare/vetch	light siliceous	autumn & spring	100		April - end Sep	20	40
red vetchling (*L. cicera*)	calc. -clay, calcareous	Sep - Oct	200		May - end Jun	18	30
winter fodder pea	gravelly	Oct	160 - 200		–	–	–
spring fodder pea	calcareous clay	Mar - Aug	200		Jun - Nov	15	25
faba bean	heavy, calcareous clay	Apr	220		May - Jun	15	35
black medick	calcareous, calc.-silic.	Sep - Oct	18 - 20		Apr - Jun following year	10	20
spring vetch	clay, calc.-clay	Mar - Jun	160 - 200		Jun - Sep	15	50
lentil	light, siliceous, gravelly	Mar - May	160		Jun - Sep	15	20
white mustard	siliceous-clay	Apr - Jul	14 - 20		Jun - end Sep	12	25
summer rape	calc.-clay, silic.-clay	–	8 - 10		–	8	20
spurrey	light, siliceous, fresh	Mar - May	35		May - end Jul	–	–
French serradella	sandy, fresh, deep	Apr - end Jul	35		Aug - end Oct	–	–
buckwheat	light, sandy	May - end Aug	60		Jul - mid Nov	–	–
gorse	barren land, silic. -clay	Apr - end Aug	15 - 20,	10	Apr - end Oct	26	12
comfrey	humic	plant Feb - Apr	by suckers		Oct onwards	20	80

* subject to change according to circumstances

Buying colonies

The hives can be filled in many ways: by artificial swarming, by buying a skep, by buying swarms.

Artificial swarming is to be preferred. It can be done when you want, at a time to suit you. It is done on colonies you know to be fit and healthy, something which is becoming rare.

When you are starting up you cannot do artificial swarms. As far as possible buy skeps. These hives will give strong swarms. Also, you can transfer them by driving at the best possible date and besides, in these hives, there is more likelihood that the colony will be healthy as well. Relative to frame beekeeping, fixed-comb beekeeping is not invaded by foul brood to the same extent.

Finally, when you have no other option, buy swarms after having made sure that their source apiary is not infested with foul brood.

Beekeepers' swarms

Beekeeper's swarms are best, and even most economical, because they are the most productive if the beekeeper practices continual selection in his beekeeping and if he delivers his swarms in good condition. In fact, the beekeeper has an interest in continually selecting in his apiary. As for those he has had delivered, they can be kept an eye on.

The time to buy

The best time to buy and hive a swarm is at the beginning of the nectar flow. At this time there is hardly any risk of having to feed the swarm; on the contrary there is every chance of seeing the colony settle down quickly, gather its stores for the winter and even, in melliferous years, giving a good harvest.

In the following months, it would only be worthwhile buying swarms in so far as the beekeeper has some completely drawn comb and stores to give them. If the production of wax costs nothing during the nectar flow, it costs a lot at other times.

The weight of the swarm

You always buy a swarm weighing 2 kg. Proportionately it costs less than a swarm of 1½ or 1 kg, since in them there is only one queen to pay for, only one lot of postage and packing.

Besides, a strong colony in a hive gives best results and largely compensates for the initial expense. It is capital invested in the society of the beehive. Such an investor will be using capital wisely and will know how to make it grow.

The swarm loses weight on the journey, because of the distance and the temperature. It is difficult to work out the original weight on arrival. The trustworthiness of the supplier is therefore of great importance.

Queen

For the presence and quality of the queen, you must depend on the honesty of the supplier.

You should always ask the supplier to proceed as I used to when I was doing breeding. The queen was shut up with some bees in a box as if she had been sent by post. The box was placed in the middle of the swarm of bees. On arrival, the buyer only has to take the box containing the queen, placing it in the hive if it is a question of getting the queen accepted. The bees will find their own way to surround the queen. In this way, the work is made easier. The bees do not escape. You can do this at any time and you will not compromise the honesty of the seller or the competence of the buyer.

Races

There are a large number of races of bees, but only two are very widespread and deserve attention: the indigenous and the Italian.

The indigenous race has a blackish-brown body; the Italian bee has two golden yellow bands around the abdomen. The Italian bee has a longer tongue, she can visit more flowers. In years of poor nectar flow, she has the advantage of the indigenous bee.

The Italian bee is more lively, more active, another quality which increases her productivity; but does this liveliness increase her nastiness? No, not if she is treated as she should be, just as the indigenous bee should be treated.

I even find the Italian bee to be more docile than the indigenous bee because she understands quicker what the beekeeper demands of her with the puffs of smoke from the smoker.

And neither do I find that this liveliness of the Italian bee makes for more robbing, so that the beekeeper at times has to reduce, as he should always do, the neighbouring hive entrances where the colonies are weak.

The Italian bee is also more prolific, even without using stimulating nourishment that is so costly and harmful. It is an important quality.

Occasionally I read that the terrible foulbrood is attributed to the Italian bee. What a mistake! On the contrary, the Italian bee has all the qualities needed to fight this disease.

Apparently, we began to recognise foulbrood at the time when Italian bees were introduced. That is possible, but it is also at the same time as the introduction of framed hives, where the bee wears itself out to no purpose. It is at the same time that the methods that add to this exhaustion were propagated. It is to bad framed hives and bad methods that we must attribute the development of foulbrood. There are no causes for its origin other than overwork and enfeeblement of the stock.

During more than twenty-five years, I have studied the most widespread bee stocks. It is the Italian race that I recommend to all beekeepers and it is of little import if they do not keep their racial purity: it is not necessary if you are not doing breeding.

In my opinion, the indigenous race suits beginners, because they will not have too much capital outlay before proving their own capability. And I am of the opinion that the indigenous race would be excellent if it was selected, as the Italian bee has been. And I must also warn beekeepers that lots of breeders, if they make, on the one hand, a selection through choice of breeding colonies, through another concern, they are, on the other hand, going against the selection that nature herself would have made.

In a queenless colony, the bees raise between 10 and 15 queens. The queen who hatches first, consequently the strongest, the most vigorous, will kill the others before they are born: it is a harsh selection.

This selection would be too costly for breeders. They isolate the royal cells before they hatch. They keep fifteen out of fifteen when nature would only keep one out of fifteen.

Nature even allows for selection at the time of the queen's fertilisation. In order to be mated the queen takes to the air and flies to a giddy height. Only the most vigorous male can reach her. If the queen from an artificial swarm is less vigorous, she can be reached by a less vigorous male. There again, is inferiority.

In practice, buy Italian bees from a breeder if you can get them from one who proceeds according to the old rules of selection and breeding, and who does not feed his bees on sugar. If not, it is best to put up with the indigenous bee. This race will soon be improved, to the point where it is better than the Italian breed of modern breeders, if you closely follow our method of destroying weak colonies and building up the best colonies through artificial swarms.

Price

The price of a swarm varies depending on the breed and its weight at the time of delivery.

In general, one estimates that a swarm of 2 kg of Italian bees is worth, at the beginning of the nectar flow, the price of 20 kg of honey (gross) postage and packing extra. This price is justified because the breeder, in selling the swarm, wipes out the production from a good colony which would have given 20 kg of honey some weeks later.

A swarm of indigenous bees is worth 25% less.

After the nectar flow, the swarm does not have the same value. Because you must envisage that:

1. You have to give it at least 100 g of syrup every day in the summer when there will not be any nectar flow so that it can build up the necessary combs for a good overwintering.
2. Furthermore, at the end of August, you have to make up the stores by occasionally providing from between 10 and 12 kg of honey.

   In contrast, if at the beginning of the nectar flow, you give a 2 kg swarm to a People's Hive, you will have a harvest in the first year, and more than in the following years, because the bees will not be held up in their work by looking after the brood, as there will not be any.
3. I should point out that to get the same result with a Dadant, you have to introduce a swarm of at least 4 kg.

A big mistake

A bee journal has published the list of breeders to whom a special allocation of sugar had been made. If these breeders really carry out a selection, this selection will be cancelled out by this abnormal food which would inevitably contribute to the weakening of the stock and set up favourable conditions for the development of illnesses, foulbrood among others.

Swarms on frames

Certain breeders supply their swarms on brood frames. This practice is not without problems.

The frames are not always exactly the same dimensions as those of the purchaser, even if he has hives of the same name – the weight of the swarm is difficult to verify. The brood does more harm than good. It is true that the brood allows the bees to raise a queen if theirs has been killed during the journey or during the hiving, but the egg-laying of this queen will be very late and the swarm will arrive in autumn with too small a population, not enough food and unfinished combs. It will be difficult for it to survive into the spring. In any case, it will not be able to prosper, even the following year.

Natural swarms

It is possible to find swarms from neighbouring beekeepers. Such swarms do not have the same value as those which come from the breeders' apiaries where selection is undertaken with knowledge and continuity.

You only need pay half the price for such swarms as you would for others.

To estimate their weight when they are hived in skeps without combs, you can use the following scale:

A swarm of 2 kg occupies 18 litres if it is hot weather, 9 litres if it is cold, and between 13 and 14 litres if the temperature is average.

You must not forget that such swarms, like the others, have their highest value only on the first day of the main nectar flow.

Skeps

To populate hives, the purchase of skeps is the simplest and often the least costly. It allows you to have a very strong swarm at the time you want with bees that are definitely healthy.

Plain swarms

The most honest sellers will rarely want to give swarms of 2 kg, because a swarm of 2 kg enfeebles their hive. They will give scarcely 1 kg 500g of bees. Now, to get a good outcome, even in the People's Hive, it is necessary to hive a swarm of 2 kg. In the Dadant hive, you need a swarm of 4 kg.

Moreover, no breeder can guarantee the shipping day. In fact, one particular day is best: it is the first day of the main nectar flow. Hived any later, the swarm will not build complete combs and will not make winter stores. You would need to feed them to keep them alive. The following year, the swarm will still not give the owner satisfaction because in the spring, they will not have built enough necessary comb for the development of brood.

In fact, after the main nectar flow, a swarm has no value.

Swarms on frames

Populating with swarms on frames has the same inconveniences as populating with plain swarms. It has other disadvantages too. The frames will not always have the necessary qualities. The wood of the frames must be carefully planed to facilitate cleaning. Between the frame uprights and the sides of the hive, there must be a gap of 7.5 mm. The frame must be positioned in such a way that this gap is never reduced or augmented. Otherwise there will be sticking and the frames will no longer be mobile. Such precision is rare.

Time

You will more easily find skeps in autumn than at any other time, especially at the time of suffocation (sulphuring); but in March you no longer run the risks of the overwintering.

Volume

Only buy large hives, which will allow for big populations before they swarm. They must be at least 30 litres, preferably 40.

A good skep would have a diameter of 300 mm with a height of 800 mm. You rarely find this. The dimensions of the skep vary according to the region.

Weight

The skep should weigh (gross) 20 kg in the autumn, if it is 40 litres, 15 kg if it is 30 litres. In March, these same hives will not weigh more than from 15 kg to about 8 kg. It is important that the combs are built right to the bottom.

Price

The price of the skep is also based on the price of the honey which it contains. A 25 kg hive contains about 12 kg 500 g of honey; a hive of 15 kg contains about 8 kg 500 g. In March, these hives will not weigh more than about 15 kg and 8 kg 500 g (gross). But they will have at least as much value as in autumn since you will not have to worry about them overwintering.

Packing

Pack up the hives towards evening, after having smoked them. Put them in a coarsely woven cloth, held in place with string. Underneath, fix some strips of wood to allow for air circulation. The tie-up is right at the bottom of the hive.

We have shown one method of packing. Here is a better one. In place of the string, use some fine pins of 40 mm which you push into the straw of the skep by hand. This procedure ensures greater adherence between the skep and the fabric (old jute sacking). There will be fewer gaps between the material and the skep, gaps where bees could be trapped and squashed or suffocated to death,

If the skep has to go by train, you pack it in wood. For that, make up two crosses from boards measuring from 100 x 100 mm of a length equal to the diameter of the skep. Join the crosses through similar boards of a length equal to the height of the skep. Wrapped up like this, the skep will be kept upside down, the opening above, thus avoiding suffocation of the bees. The address and 'live bees' labels are then fixed on afterwards. In these conditions, only violent shocks to the skep will be a matter of concern.

Packing

Transport

Transport of skeps must be undertaken with gentleness and care.

For preference, they should be sent by hand, in any case in soft-sprung vehicles.

If it is possible, there will be fewer breaks in the comb if they are lined up in the direction of travel.

The hives must be put down in the evening in the place where they are going to stay. Cut the string and allow the cloth to fall. Next day remove the cloth. While waiting till you are able to put the hives in place, keep them in the shade, preferably in a cool and dark place.

It is best to transport skeps in the autumn. Because from January onwards, travel has the same effect as stimulatory feeding. It can provoke an early swarm and prevent driving (transferring) the bees at a good moment.

Installing the skep

Very occasionally, skeps have a capacity of 40 litres. In such cases, in order to avoid a spring-like swarming before driving the bees, it is good to place the skep on a hive-body box with wax starter, or better still, a box with drawn comb if you have one. Because skeps come in different sizes which do not conform to the square of our hive-body boxes, you will find it better to use our special adapter board which fits on a hive-body box and can take skeps of any size. To resume: on an ordinary floor, place a box with starter or drawn comb. On this box put our special board. Place the skep in the very centre of this board. Then cover the whole thing with a roof, with tarred paper etc. to protect it from the rain. If there are bee spaces between the skep and the special floor/board, close them up with daub, mortar etc. You now have only to wait for when the bees are driven (transferred).

Feeding

If on the arrival of the skep you find that it weighs only 18 kg at the end of October or 15 kg in February, you must feed it. For that, before installing the skep, you place a small feeder on the ordinary hive floor, under the box. You use this feeder when the temperature allows, and as soon as the state of the colony demands it. Do not forget that the small feeder can only be used when the bees go out during the day.

If it is necessary to feed in cold weather, you must employ other means. Fill a small bottle with syrup. Close the neck with some fine material tied on with string. Make a hole in the top of the skep and place the upside-down bottle into it.

If the skep weighs very much more, it will have the grave disadvantage of not leaving enough space for the development of the spring brood. In that case a box with drawn comb becomes essential.

This populated skep will give a swarm of between 2 and 3 kg of healthy bees.

Illnesses are rare in skeps. You will be able to drive the bees into a new hive to suit on the first day of the main nectar flow, since you will have it to hand. For this reason, in its first year, three months after its hiving, it will give an abundant harvest, all the more so because, if you have followed my advice, you will have practised the method which I call 'pioneering'.

Driven bees

Several manuals advise populating hives with driven bees saved from suffocation/sulphuring (*chasse* or *trévas*).

To succeed in forming a good colony with these bees, there are several conditions.

First you must have at your disposal, for each driven colony, two complete boxes of drawn comb, and upwards of 12 kg of stores, preferably of honey, stores that will quickly be taken in. It is thus necessary to operate in September, because in October there will not always be very many warm days where the bees will be in a condition to take in the stores. It is also necessary to operate with strong colonies, because there will not be any brood to increase the number of bees, nor to replace those which will be killed during the operation.

It is true that you can often unite two driven colonies. But in this case it is necessary to kill one of the two queens. In order to do that you use our queen cage. This operation is described further on. But how do we get the bees from the skep? By beating, as we described in the section 'Driving (transferring) bees'. This will rarely be possible in September. The temperature will not be warm enough. Besides, the owner of the skep will not always allow beating, because it spoils his hive.

That leaves temporary asphyxiation. Here is how you proceed in order to asphyxiate the bees:

Place 2 g potassium nitrate in a bowl, and add enough water to dissolve the salt. Put some old bits of cloth in the liquid, some pieces of old sack, enough to absorb all the liquid. Dry the fabric at some distance from any heat source, as it can catch fire easily. Set light to the cloths below the skep after having covered them with a metal sheet so that the bees do not fall into the flames. Lightly tap the hive to make the bees fall. Lift the hive and gather the bees. If there is significant piling-up of bees, spread them out so that they can breathe straight away and will not drown in their excrement, because the potassium nitrate will have given them violent diarrhoea. Work as quickly as possible throughout this operation.

Natural swarms

It often happens that natural swarms establish themselves in the hollows of trees, in old thick walls, etc. How do we take them?

Operate at the beginning of the main nectar flow. Make two openings if there are none: one at the top of the place occupied by the swarm, the other below. Above the top opening, place a box, a People's Hive box. Smoke through the lower opening until all the bees have come out. In the box you have a swarm which you deal with in the same way as any other. Afterwards you harvest the honey and the wax that the bees have left, without bothering with the brood. This work is rarely remunerative.

In the evening, the swarm must be transported at least 3 km away, if not, the bees, at least the old ones, will return to the site.

You can place the swarm nearer to its original place if at first you keep it in a cellar for three days before it is hived. In that case give it a little food.

You can also collect passing natural swarms. For that, you place some hives or preferably bait hives high up, near the apiary or near a wood etc. In the hive you place several old combs. It is good to rub the inside of the hive with a clump of melissa or with some propolis dissolved in methylated spirits.

If these swarms are weak, or arrive late, you must feed them so that they can build comb and afterwards complete their winter stores.

Preparation of the hive

So that beekeeping tasks are quick and easy, it is important that the combs are straight and pointing in the same direction. To ensure this is the case, it is necessary to put a wax starter-strip of about 5 mm under the top-bar.

Here is how to proceed in putting the starter on the top-bar.

First method

Make a lath the length of the starter to be made. Its planed size is 15 mm thick and 24 mm wide. In the middle of the width nail two thin, long pins.

Obtain a pan to melt the wax and a calligraphy brush. Put a bit of water in the pan so the wax does not burn then add the required amount of wax.

Obtain a sponge and a basin in which is dissolved one part of honey to two parts of cold water.

Step 1: take the lath and wet it with the sponge soaked in honey-water.

Step 2: take a top-bar. Be careful not to wet it, otherwise the wax will not stick to it.

Step 3: fit the lath on the top-bar so that the two pins rest against one of the sides of the top-bar. In this way, one of the sides of the lath will be in the middle of the width of the top-bar.

Step 4: dip the brush in the melted wax, move it rapidly along the interior side of the lath and the middle of the top-bar, and repeat this several times.

Step 5: remove the lath

Step 6: turn the top-bar round and pass several strokes of the waxed brush along the other side of the starter.

Comment

The more passes with the brush, the thicker the starter strip.

Second method

Prepare a lath-template with pins to hold the top-bar and cover it as far as its centre. Place the top-bar B against the template A (see diagram), which should always be moistened. Hold all of it in the left hand and slope it from back to front as in C . Using a spoon in the right hand, pour a little liquid wax on the top-bar, as in C. When the wax has set sufficiently, remove the top-bar with its starter-strip D; run a little wax down the other side of the starter, then place the top-bar in the hive-body box.

This is our preferred method.

It helps to have several templates, especially in summer. They cool while work continues. The result is better and proceeds more rapidly.

Once the top-bars are thus in place they are fixed in the rebate with a small headless pin such as a glazier's pin.

We prefer this method to fixing with toothed racks or bent nails, or having ends of top-bars of 36 mm wide. The latter constitute an expense and make cleaning very difficult. They look good when they emerge from the workshop, but no longer so when they come out of the hive.

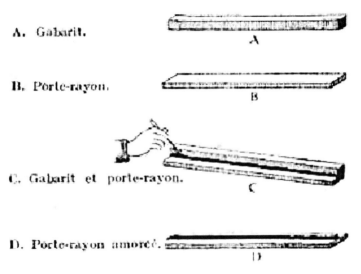

A. Gabarit.

B. Porte-rayon.

C. Gabarit et porte-rayon.

D. Porte-rayon amorcé.

A. Template for putting starter-strips on top-bars. B. Top-bar.
C. Template and top-bar. D. Top-bar with starter strip of wax.

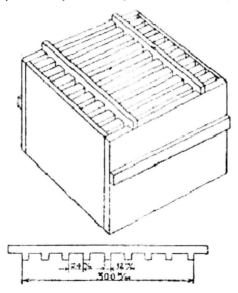

Template for positioning the top-bars and retaining them while nailing.

Third method

This method is a lot simpler but it requires top-bars that are more difficult to make (see illustration).

The top-bar has a tongue like tongue-and-groove flooring. The tongue should be only 3–4 mm tall and right in the centre of the top-bar.

The top-bar is bevelled. Again, it is important to position the ridge of the bevel in the middle of the top-bar and make its projection 3–4 mm below the bottom edges of the sides.

To put wax starter on these two top-bars it is sufficient to brush the projecting parts with melted wax. Thereafter the top-bars need only a rough cleaning. They will always be sufficiently impregnated with wax.

78

However, I should warn that these two top-bars slightly increase the waste space between each storey of top-bars, which is a defect, as we have said.

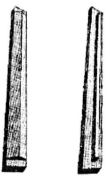

Ridged top-bars

Fourth method

Top-bars can also be fitted with strips of foundation, if some is available, though better still with plain wax that can be made oneself.

These strips of wax can be fixed to the top-bars in different ways. A groove could be cut in the top-bar, the wax strip inserted, and both sides stuck to the bar by running a little melted wax along them. As a result, this groove is difficult to clean out. We prefer to proceed otherwise.

Place the wax strip in the middle of the top-bar and hold it in place with the fingers or a rod. Run a little melted wax from the side that is exposed. Remove the rod and run a little wax from the other side.

Here are two methods for making wax starter strips.

Method 1: Make a well-planed wooden rod with a length of 290 mm, a thickness of approximately 10 mm and a width of 15 mm. Oil this wooden rod or briefly dip it in water. Quickly immerse the wooden rod in melted wax once or several times and remove it immediately. The rod can be held by two nails or pins placed at its ends. When the wax round the rod has cooled sufficiently, cut the wax off the whole width of the wooden rod. There remains on each flat surface of the rod a strip of wax of 15 mm x 290 mm. The cooler the molten wax the thicker the wax strips. The more times the wooden rod is dipped in the wax, the thicker the wax strips. Usually a thickness of 2 mm is sufficient.

If wax or a receptacle of a sufficient volume is not available, a shorter wooden rod can be used which produces shorter wax strips. But several can be placed end to end.

Do not forget to melt the wax in a bain-marie.

Method 2: Put some cold water in a flat bottomed bottle (Vichy or Vittel type).

Drench the bottle with cold soapy water placed in a bucket and wipe it lightly with the hand, i.e. without a cloth, to remove excess water.

Dip the bottle in melted wax for one or two seconds and remove. One then obtains on the bottle a thin layer of wax which is easy to thicken by repeating the operation several times in succession, at a sufficient speed such that the preceding layers do not melt.

Using a knife, detach the bottom of the wax adhering to the bottom of the bottle, dip the latter in cold, clean water, and detach the wax by cutting along the length of the bottle. Do not forget to dip the bottle in soapy water each time a new sheet is started. The depth of the sheet is determined by how deeply the bottle is dipped in the wax. The bottoms cut off are not useable and are re-melted.

Note

It is important that the undersides of the top-bars are always rough, i.e. unplaned, so as to facilitate the adherence of the wax.

Beekeeping procedures

Before going into the beekeeping procedures carried out during the course of the year, we must give some words of advice. If they are observed, you will come to work quickly without stings and will always have gentle bees. For, do not forget that it is with their full agreement that bees give honey. The reason why they are obliged to use their sting is because they have been allowed to believe that we are their enemy: *'sponte faons, aegre spicuta'*.

Helper

All beekeeping tasks can be performed alone but it is often necessary in such circumstances to put the smoker down or work with only one hand. It is also necessary to stop to deal with the smoker. As a result the work is slower and bees end up by getting annoyed.

So it is better to have a helper who keeps the smoker going and who can smoke the bees more gently, because it can be done continuously.

Tool-box

The beekeeper should be accompanied by a tool-box. He will find in this box all he needs for his work: rolls for the smoker, hive-tool etc. In this box he will also place, and without danger of robbing, the fragments of comb, the scrapings, wax, honey and even propolis. All this debris, if left accessible to the bees will attract them and provoke robbing.

Stands

When the beekeeper handles the hive-bodies he will equip himself with stands to put the boxes on the ground. Otherwise there is a danger of squashing the bees and getting the underside of the boxes dirty, which would then require cleaning.

This would result in time wastage and danger of hurting and annoying the bees.

Veil

All beekeeping work may be carried out without wearing a veil. However, the beekeeper and his helper must nevertheless keep a veil close at hand to use in case of accident.

Novice beekeepers should always wear a veil. They will have greater steadiness. They will do without it later when they are experienced with bees.

Smoker

It is possible to perform some operations without a smoker. But people are always wrong to do it this way. In doing so, they always annoy the bees, which is something that should be avoided.

The smoker is for warning the bees, calming them, directing them, in a word, for speaking to them.

You may take the attitude that you will not use a smoker; you would be making a mistake nonetheless.

A pipe, cigar or cigarette can often replace a smoker.

The smoke warns the bees that something is about to happen. Prudently, they eat honey. Assured of having food at their disposal, they are less aggressive. Perhaps the honey inside them stops them bending as easily to insert their sting.

Silence

The operator will chat as little as possible during his work. In this way, all his attention will be on his work. He will work quicker and better remember the observations he made during his work and take note of them.

Gentleness and speed

The beekeeper must try to be gentle in the vicinity of his bees; gentle in the manipulation of the smoker and the boxes; gentle in his words and movements.

The bees respond to the beekeeper's gentleness with gentleness. Furthermore, the beekeeper will tend to become expeditious, but without stopping being gentle and without becoming rough or violent, for long manipulations annoy the bees and certainly cool the brood.

Propolis

Propolis often prevents the beekeeper from being gentle and expeditious. Propolis inside the boxes cannot hinder our work because we almost never touch the interior. It is not the same thing with the propolis between the boxes on the rims of the walls and on the top-bars above the combs.

Each time we open a box we must pass the hive tool along the rims of the walls and top-bars. The propolis is put into a compartment in the toolbox, to avoid risk of robbing, however small.

The hive tool is well suited to this task.

Robbing

If a piece of comb or simply a little propolis is allowed to fall on the ground, the neighbouring bees come to look for the small amount of honey that is there. The bees of the hive being worked on then defend their property and fighting breaks out. The bees then try to enter neighbouring hives to continue to gather honey. The fighting increases. And during the heat of battle everyone becomes an enemy: bees, beekeepers, passers-by and even the most peaceable animals.

Angry colonies

As a result of accidents, children throwing stones, etc., one may come across angry colonies that are difficult to approach. Here are some methods of calming them. Apparently they are always successful.

First method: Open the hive. With a spray containing clean water douse the colony lightly. This light rain sticks the wings of the bees and impairs their movement. Cover the hive and a quarter of an hour later you may proceed normally. However, only use this method if the temperature is 20–25°.

Second method: An hour before the hive opening, move the hive some distance away. Put an empty hive in its place. This hive will receive the old bees, the worst tempered. Work on your hive and then replace it after having moved the hive with the old bees to one side. These will then return to their hive.

I have never had to use these methods, doubtless because with the People's Hive there is never a need to carry out major operations inside the hive.

Stings

If by chance you are stung by a bee, it is advisable to try any of the following: sucking out the venom; ammonia solution; sodium hypochlorite solution (bleach); rubbing it with pear leaves or parsley leaves.

First task

In every beekeeping operation, the first task is to send two or three puffs of smoke into the hive entrance.

Second task

In every beekeeping operation, the second task should be to wait for the sound of the bees humming before opening the hive.

Populating the hive

A new hive can be populated with a colony from a variety of sources. Accordingly, the method of doing so varies somewhat.

With swarms from breeders

Work in the evening towards sunset. Stand beside the site to receive the colony and proceed as for a transfer (driving bees).

But before starting, smoke the bees. Then place the box containing the swarm under the first box of the hive after removing its covering (instead of the skep that you see inverted in a bucket in the illustration, see p. 85). Then, instead of beating the box with the swarm, as would be the case with a skep, send smoke through the mesh vents. You will see the bees climb up. You proceed thereafter as described for driving bees.

With natural swarms

Do this also in the evening, at sunset. Place the swarm right by the site that the colony will occupy and proceed as for transferring (driving) bees from a skep containing wax and bees, or as we show on the engraving below.

With skeps

This method of populating hives is so frequent, above all with novices, that we have devoted a special section to it: transferring (driving) bees.

The swarm has been received in a skep. An hour before sunset, no earlier, the beekeeper carries the swarm to its final place. He inverts the hive-body box so that it is open at the top. He vigorously shakes the skep to detach the bees and pours them into a People's Hive as he would grain. If there are bees left in the skep he shakes it again and again pours the bees into the People's Hive. For a breeder's swarm received in a swarm box, the beekeeper may proceed in the same way after having removed the lid or the bottom of the box. A completely empty hive-body box is placed on the hive to serve as a funnel. This is removed after the operation.

Driving (transferring) bees

Several methods of transferring or driving bees are recommended. But we will present only one.

No superimposition

Superimposition, placing one hive above the other, should ideally be used in March, because in this month it is easier to reduce the height of the basket and combs. This ensures the reliability of the method.

Despite this precaution, if the nectar flow is insufficient, the bees stay in the skep and do not enter the new hive. Even in melliferous years, the installation of bees in a new hive is often inadequate. After the harvest, it is necessary to feed them in order to make-up their stores and also to make them build comb. Add to that the fact that with this method it is a long and difficult task to monitor the combs when the bees are building them. As a result, this way, instead of saving time, in fact wastes it. It complicates the work instead of simplifying it and often fails to achieve the aim intended.

No driving at all in March

Transfer should not be done in March. At this time, driving the bees is slow and difficult. It also causes the brood to be chilled. One is often obliged to use asphyxia. And in addition, would not putting brood in a large, cold hive containing a handful of bees risk this brood dying of cold, at least part of it? This could lead to foulbrood in the apiary, or at least it would definitely retard brood development.

Date and time of driving

Bees should be transferred when the main nectar flow has begun. Moreover, the date cannot be fixed because it varies from year to year and from place to place. It is clear when the nectar flow has begun when a few kilos of honey are seen coming into the hive. This can be verified by hefting the hives or when there are natural swarms in the area.

If it is done too early, a useful brood is lost and it causes production of brood that hinders yield. Also, one is often obliged to feed it. If it is done too late, part of the nectar flow is lost.

The operation is done on a fine day after a preceding day of fine weather, between 11 a.m. and 3 p.m., preferably at 11 a.m.

Never total transfer

When bees are transferred by driving, only the bees should be used. The brood will be destroyed; the honey and the wax is used as at harvest time. The brood retains workers in the hive and stops them taking part in the nectar flow. It is thus only a disadvantage to transfer the brood too.

Leaving the brood in the skep with a few bees or giving this brood some bees from another colony by exchanging places just increases the number of weak colonies. For two weak colonies never produce as much as one strong colony. In the two weak colonies there are two groups of bees kept at the hive for cleaning it and incubating and feeding the brood. In a strong colony, a single group is retained for each of the three aforementioned jobs inside the hive.

Furthermore, when the nectar flow is over, if you have honey, it will be easy for you, as we will describe, to make increase with less difficulty and less risk, using artificial swarming.

Method

To transfer bees by driving, carry out all of the procedures indicated below.

Note well that this should be done:

– at the start of the nectar flow;

– in fine weather;

– from 11 a.m. to 3 p.m. (solar time);

and that you should prepare in advance a hive comprising at least two boxes; a bucket or receptacle of some kind able to receive the skep; four sticks.

1. Moving the skep of bees to be driven: The helper very gently sends some smoke into the skep. When the bees are humming, the beekeeper takes the basket and moves it some distance so as not to be inconvenienced by the foragers or bees from neighbouring colonies, and places it upside down on a bucket, an empty hive body, a box or a tub. It is important that the helper smokes the bees as little as possible during this procedure (Fig. 1, see p. 85).

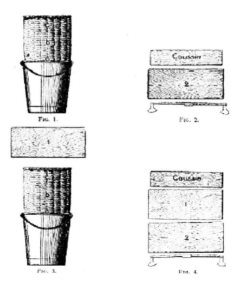

Fig. 1. Fig. 2.

Fig. 3. Fig. 4.

2. Installation of the new hive: Where the skep was, the beekeeper and helper place a hive comprising a floor, the second hive-body box and the quilt (Fig. 2). During the procedure, this hive will receive the foragers from the skep.

3. Placement of one hive-body box on the skep of bees to be driven: The helper smokes the bees sufficiently to avoid them getting angry, neither more nor less. The beekeeper places the first hive body on the skep of bees to be driven. Provisionally, until the first inspection, the cloth over the top-bars of this box is attached with pins (Fig. 3).

4. Beating: The beekeeper and his helper sit at right-angles next to the skep so as to be able to beat it in four different places, although at the same height. They have a watch near them. They beat near the bottom of the skep in A (formerly the top of the skep) for three minutes. Then the beekeeper and his helper beat for three minutes higher up, in B, in the middle of the skep. Finally, they beat for three minutes, in C, almost near the rim of the skep.

5. Putting the populated hive-body box in place: If the operation has been done in the way we described, after this beating for nine minutes, the bees will have climbed into the hive-body box. The beekeeper takes the box with the bees and carries it to its final position, avoiding any shaking. The helper removes the quilt covering the second box and puffs the smoker into it gently. The beekeeper places the first box on the second. The helper puts the quilt back on the two boxes (Fig. 4) and then the roof.

6. Dismantling the skep from which the bees were driven: The beekeeper and his helper return immediately to the skep from which the bees were driven. The beekeeper lifts it up and the helper smokes it abundantly, especially if he notices robbers present. The skep is dismantled in a place inaccessible to bees. The honey is extracted. The wax is rendered as soon as possible and the brood destroyed.

Note

To check for the presence of the queen, before putting the first hive-body box on the second, the beekeeper puts it down for a few seconds on a dark-coloured cloth. When he lifts it up he will notice white eggs on the cloth which confirm the presence of the queen.

Driving bees from a framed hive

Instead of a skep, one may have a framed hive to drive bees from. Here is how to proceed.

First case: You are familiar with the queen and your frames are still mobile. Move the hive some distance. Find the queen. At midday the queen is always at one side or other of the brood nest, one day to the right, the other to the left. Using a bee brush, sweep the queen with her bees into the new hive. Move gently and with care. Immediately take all the frames one by one and quickly sweep all the bees into the new hive.

Second case: You are not familiar with the queen or the frames are not mobile. Move the hive some distance. Leave it there. Put a hive-body box of the People's Hive on top of it as before. Cover the parts of the framed hive, which are not covered by the box, using paper or cardboard. Beat as for a skep and, in addition, puff smoke copiously in at the entrance.

Rating colonies

Time

Rating colonies takes place in April in the Paris region, after two or three days of fine weather, at a temperature of 12–15°, and between 11 a.m. and 2 p.m.

Procedure

After a few seconds of observation you write on a card the number of each colony under two headings:

Good colonies – those where you see bees returning with their legs loaded with pollen.

Colonies under observation – those where you do not see bees coming and going and those where you see bees entering, but without pollen on their legs.

The colonies of the first category will be subjected to the 'spring visit' (see next section), as soon as possible and at no matter what temperature. The colonies of the second category are observed again eight days after the first visit and classified. The good colonies will in their turn be subjected to the spring visit.

The inspection of the other colonies is carried out as follows.

Inspection of doubtful colonies

The helper puffs smoke into the entrance of the hive. Then the beekeeper, after removing the roof and quilt, peels back the cloth. Finally, while the helper smokes the top of the top box gently, the beekeeper scrapes the top-bars and the rim of the box with the hive tool to remove the propolis.

First case: During the operation, you see a cluster of bees in the hive. Replace the cloth and the quilt and proceed directly with the spring cleaning, i.e. cleaning the floor. If in eight days you see no more pollen coming in to this hive, dispense with this colony using the method described in the section 'Getting ready for winter'.

Second case: In proceeding as described in the first case, you do not find a cluster of bees in the hive. Conclude that this colony has died out. A few bees scattered here and there on the combs may be ignored.

This hive is cleaned. Its combs, if they are in good condition, are used if need be, otherwise they are protected from robbers and wax moths as described in the section 'Getting ready for winter'.

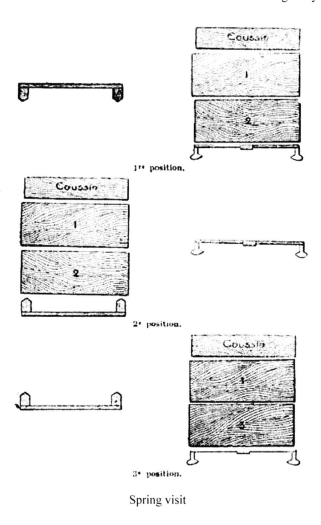

Spring visit

Spring visit

Nothing to do inside the hive

Each box of the People's Hive comes into the beekeeper's hands at least once every three years. When this happens it can be easily and thoroughly cleaned.

As a result, cleaning the brood chamber is unnecessary. It would even be harmful because it would greatly cool the brood chamber. You should therefore refrain from cleaning the brood chamber, even avoid opening it without reason.

At the time of the spring visit, enlargement of the hive can be initiated.

87

Cleaning the floor

The floor needs cleaning. Moreover, it can be cleaned without danger of chilling the brood chamber. To clean the floor proceed as follows:

1. The beekeeper places a hive-body box stand near the hive. The helper gently puffs a little smoke into the entrance. When the bees are humming, the beekeeper lifts the roof then takes the two boxes without removing the quilt and puts them on the stand. The helper smokes under the boxes and more strongly on the floor if there are bees there.

2. The beekeeper cleans the floor with a hive-tool. The helper cleans the support for the floor. The beekeeper puts the floor back in place and checks that it is level.

3. The helper gently puffs a little smoke under the two boxes. The beekeeper lifts the two boxes, still covered with the quilt, ready to put them back on the floor.

4. The helper smokes more strongly under the two boxes, and especially on the floor, to avoid crushing the bees. The beekeeper replaces the two boxes on the floor cold-way.

Cold-way and warm-way

Warm-way and cold-way is determined by the orientation of the combs.

In warm-way the combs are perpendicular to the walls to the right and left of the hive. With this orientation, the air coming in by the entrance meets the combs and cools the hive down less rapidly. Warm-way is the winter orientation.

In cold-way the combs are at right angles to the walls at the front and back of the hive. With this orientation, the air that comes in the entrance immediately penetrates between the combs without meeting any obstacle and cools the hive more rapidly. Cold-way is the summer orientation.

The design of the People's Hive allows warm-way or cold-way to be chosen at will.

State of the stores

In a well managed apiary there is no need to deal with the stores at the spring visit. The bee is economical. She never consumes more than necessary, as we know.

However, if you are uncertain whether your bees have what they need, it is absolutely necessary that you assess the stores as soon as possible on the first fine day. If you see that the colonies lack stores, or if you know that they have only insufficient stores, you must feed them before the stores are exhausted.

However, feed as late as possible, because feeding in spring is always harmful and all the more harmful for being done earlier.

It is equally important to give the colonies double what they are lacking, for feeding produces an increase in the brood and demands a supplementary production of heat. Finally, it is important to feed quickly, thus preferably with the large feeder.

Enlarging the hive

Bees need more space in summer to house the brood and honey, and also to reduce the effect of heat. If they lack space, they swarm. As a result, the honey harvest is reduced.

Timing

In the People's Hive we need have no fear of chilling the brood, so we must initiate enlargement soon enough to avoid swarming. This enlargement is thus done at least five days before the nectar flow. It can even be done at the spring visit, in the Easter holidays, for example, if you have more time to spare then.

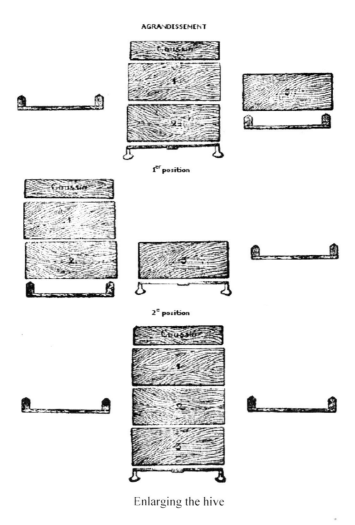

Enlarging the hive

Number of hive-body boxes

The People's Hive always has two boxes. At the time of enlargement it is necessary to add one or more according to the strength of the colony. The number of bees which enter and leave indicates the strength of the colony.

Therefore classify the hives into two groups, average and strong. The weak ones were removed in autumn. In regions where the average harvest is between 15 kg and 20 kg per hive, one box is added immediately to average colonies and two boxes to strong ones.

In regions where the average harvest is between 20 kg and 30 kg per hive, two boxes are added to average colonies and three to strong ones.

Obviously these boxes can be added at different times with an interval of some days in between, provided that you ensure that the bees do not lack space. Furthermore, it can happen that this number of boxes is not enough. I have had Peoples' Hives with seven boxes.

Adding a box

To add a box, proceed as follows:

1. The helper, after having prepared the third box (3, see p. 89), gently puffs a little smoke in the hive (1, 2). When the bees are humming, the beekeeper removes the roof.

2. The beekeeper takes the two boxes with the quilt and places them on a hive-body box stand. The helper smokes under the boxes and even more strongly on the floor, if there are bees there, so as to avoid crushing them. The beekeeper takes the third box, empty of bees, but prepared with starter strips, and puts it on the floor cold-way.

3. The helper gently puffs a little smoke under the two boxes (1, 2). The beekeeper picks up the two boxes to place them cold-way on the empty box (3).

Monitoring the apiary

The apiary, where the spring visit and enlargement of hives will have taken place in conditions we have already indicated, can be left to itself without any great harm.

You may lose a swarm here or there. You will nevertheless get a good honey harvest.

However, those who can do so, without great expense, will always benefit from keeping an eye on the hives from time to time. Two things can be observed: whether the arrival and departure of the bees is normal; whether the bees are forming beards.

Arrival and departure of bees

There is a steady to and fro of bees which increases as the season advances. Some of them are carrying pollen.

If it is like this you can conclude without opening the hive that all is well inside.

The bees make a beard

In this case there is a risk of swarming and it is important to take immediate remedial action.

First of all, check that the hive is well shaded, well protected from the midday sun and that it has enough boxes.

Then, if necessary, exchange hive positions and, if required, ventilate.

Exchanging hive positions

An apiary often has an exceptionally strong colony. It requires lots of boxes. I prefer to exchange its position with a less strong colony. One then obtains only colonies of equal strength.

Exchanging positions of hives is done in the evening after sunset. Both colonies are lightly smoked and the roofs and quilts are removed. The operation requires two people. Each passes a rope round two legs of the hive and ties the ends of the rope at a level of a decimetre below the hands such that the height of the person does not prevent the hive from being kept horizontal. This way transporting is easy.

Ventilation

In very hot weather, especially if the hives are not very well shaded from the sun, addition of boxes or exchanging hives does not always stop bees forming a beard. In which case it is necessary to ventilate the hive by facilitating the escape of hot air. For this, make three strips of wood from an old top-bar. Place two or three of the strips of wood on two or three top-bars of the top box, at the back, under the roof, covering the width of the wall of the hive. Replace the cloth, quilt and roof, but in such a way that the roof does not hinder the escape of hot air from the hive. To achieve this it is sufficient to pull it as far back as possible.

Weak swarms

During the course of summer you may have occasion to take small swarms. These swarms have to be fed each day where there is not enough nectar flow and at the rate of 100 grammes of syrup per day. Our small feeder serves perfectly for this feeding.

For, it is important that by autumn these swarms will have two boxes completely full of comb. The stores may be completed in the autumn but the comb can no longer be constructed.

Ants

Ants occasionally invade the hive. To prevent them doing so, place the hive legs in tins containing a liquid of some kind or surround the legs with a band soaked in thick grease.

Section honey

Sections are generally not profitable, because, according to my estimate, it costs three times that of extracted honey. But it may happen that beekeepers will find some takers at that price.

In any case, sections allow beekeepers to make more attractive presents, or to satisfy their own taste.

Section equipment

Now, the People's Hive, with its fixed combs, is better than all others for rapid construction of beautiful sections.

To do this, it is first necessary to construct a special box. The depth should be that of the sections used and the internal dimensions such that there is no empty space round the sections and that they match as closely as possible the internal dimensions of the hive bodies.

It is not necessary that the dimensions of these boxes are exactly the same. And here is how to do it.

The hives are enlarged as normal. When the nectar flow has really started, i.e. when there is already a small amount of honey stored in the top box, at least 5 kg, this box, which we refer to as box number one, is lifted. The following box (No. 2) is lifted likewise. On the next box (No. 3) is placed

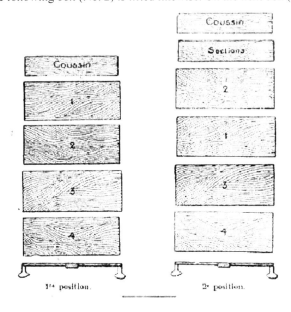

box No. 1 whose honey has been uncapped if necessary. On box No. 1 is placed box No. 2. On box No. 2 is placed the box containing sections (see figure; coussin=quilt).

Equipment for section honey

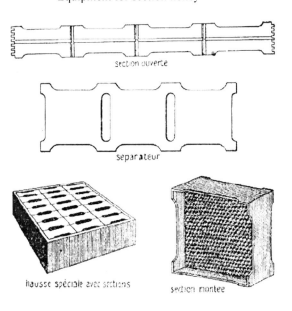

(section open, separator, section rack, assembled section)

92

Under the box containing the sections there is some brood and as a result of this no room for the honey that is brought in daily. The bees are therefore forced to put the new honey in the sections.

Furthermore, the bees never leave honey for long under brood. The bees will thus have a tendency to carry honey from box No. 1 into that containing the sections. There is therefore a rapid and considerable influx of honey into the sections. This is all that is necessary to obtain beautiful sections.

And note that here our bees are not pushed into swarming as happens in other hives when one makes sections. For, in the People's Hive one can always leave a free space for the bees under the brood, in box No. 3, and as much of it as one can give to them if the need is felt.

Note

In sections, a simple starter is sufficient and gives more even sections.
Sections should be monitored. They should be removed as soon as they are capped.

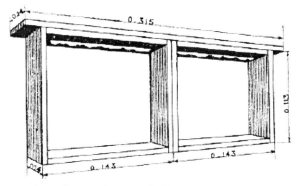

To insert American sections, fix two frames of 142 x 113 mm to a top-bar. Place eight top-bars equipped thus in a hive-body box of 130 mm deep instead of 210 mm.

The nectar flow

Certainly, the main aim of beekeeping is to produce honey. But what is required for bees installed in a hive to be able to fill it with honey?

Flowers

Flowers are the principal source of nectar. There is nectar on the leaves of certain plants, vetch, salsify, etc., and of certain trees: oak, ash, lime, etc.

Temperature

Temperature plays a very important part in the production of honey. If the temperature is favourable, there is even nectar on leaves. If the temperature is not favourable there is no nectar anywhere, not even in flowers.

A warm temperature (20°) is necessary for nectar production. Soil and atmospheric moisture increases it. Drought or thundery weather impedes it. The most favourable wind is that from the south-west. The north wind, on the other hand, stops nectar from rising.

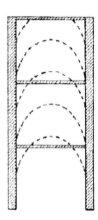

Cross-section of three boxes: the dotted lines show the successive positions of the honey according to how much is brought in, starting at the top. The brood descends accordingly.

Nectar

The honey we consume is not what is brought in by bees foraging.

Nectar, when it leaves the flower, contains up to 75% water. This is why it is called nectar at that point, to distinguish it from honey, which should contain only 20–25% water.

The water in nectar evaporates under the influence of the temperature and the ventilation produced by the bees.

Placement of nectar

On re-entering the hive, the foragers deposit the nectar anywhere, to save time, and to favour evaporation. But as soon as they have time and the opportunity, they carry the nectar to its final position, above and beside the brood. They never leave it for long below.

Pioneering method

Brood is disadvantageous during the nectar flow

The brood retains in the hive many bees that could otherwise go foraging. This is why many beekeepers have tried by various means to reduce or even get rid of the brood during this period. The methods used have often been disastrous, because they went against the laws of nature. Sometimes too, they have not given the expected results because they were carried out at a certain amount of time before the nectar flow. Now, it is impossible to specify the precise date of the nectar flow; the temperature brings it forward or delays it.

A good method

When driving bees from a skep, we recommend that the brood be destroyed. If, of course, this operation is carried out at the start of the nectar flow, it provides an opportunity to effect this removal without extra work and with every chance of getting a good result. Now, this removal of brood can be done on all colonies.

At the start of the main nectar flow, when the first sainfoin flowers appear in countries where it is cultivated, all the bees are made to go down into empty boxes with starter strips. All the brood is destroyed and the honey and wax is harvested. If during the following three days the bees are not at all able to go out, it is necessary to feed them. That is the risk of the method, a very low risk. Without this mischance, the bees, like stalwart reapers and without offspring, will obtain a more substantial harvest.

Of course it will be necessary to provide this colony with as many boxes with starter strips as one has removed of built comb.

Making increase

To increase the number of colonies in an apiary, the same methods can be used as for populating the hive: breeders' swarms, natural swarms, skeps. Artificial swarming can be used too.

This is discussed in the section 'Population of the hive'.

We are going to say a word, however, about natural swarms and then about how to make an artificial swarm.

Natural swarm

Its ownership

If you notice the departure of a swarm from your apiary or that of another beekeeper, follow it. Whatever property it enters, nobody can refuse you entry. When the swarm has settled somewhere, take possession of it by positioning next to it a person who takes your place or an object that belongs to you. This swarm belongs to you. You may do what is necessary with it where it is settled. You are only liable to someone else for any damage that you may have caused them.

How to forecast it

The bees make a beard at the entrance of the hive, because the hive has become too small as a result of the increase in population or the ambient temperature.

One often hears the piping of the young queens. At the entrance of the hive, early in the morning, there is an unusual buzz. The males make a characteristic humming noise.

A swarm may leave between two downpours or after a thunderstorm, between 8 a.m. and 4 p.m.. The departure may be delayed if the wind is strong or if the barometer indicates heavy rain.

How to make a swarm settle

Using a mirror, shine a shaft of sunlight onto the swarm, or even spray the swarm with a fine rain using a powerful garden syringe. The swarm will cluster immediately and land on the first tree it comes to.

How to take a swarm

Let the swarm cluster and prepare a hive-body box. Scorch this box so as to destroy any insects and spider webs and to increase the smell of wax, if it has already been used. Moisten the walls of the box with a few drops of honey.

When the swarm is properly clustered, lightly smoke it. Wear a veil. Place the box with the opening upwards directly below the swarm. Sharply knock the branch on which the swarm has settled once or twice. Turn the box the right way up and place it on a hive-body box stand.

If the bees are fanning their wings around the box and tending to go into it, your operation is successful and you can go away.

If not, especially if the bees are returning to the branch where the swarm was in increasing numbers, wait until the swarm has re-clustered there and repeat the procedure. In the following pages, we show various locations of swarms and indicate how to take them.

The beekeeper drives bees with smoke into a People's Hive placed above them.
In the evening he carries the hive to its final position.

96

Hiving

If the swarm has to be hived at least three kilometres away, it should be taken to its final site during the first evening, around sunset.

It is advisable to scorch the new hive so as to remove any unpleasant smell, and then rub it inside and out with *Melissa officinale* or mint.

Feeding

If the nectar flow stops for more than two days, it will be necessary to feed the swarm as generously as possible, for it needs nourishment and to draw comb.

The beekeeper knocks the branch to drop the bees into a People's Hive, then the helper turns it the right way up and puts it on a hive-body box stand. In the evening it is carried to its final position.

The beekeeper brushes the bees down into a People's Hive, then the helper turns it the right way up and puts it on a hive-body box stand. In the evening it is carried to its final position.

97

Artificial swarming

Use

Artificial swarming is a very efficient way of populating hives.

Waiting for natural swarms is sometimes a long drawn out affair. In any case, such swarms cannot always be guaranteed to stay in the hive.

Buying swarms is an expense that is not always cost efficient and does not always give bees of good quality.

When

The best time to artificial swarm is at the beginning of the main nectar flow when natural swarms start to be seen in the region.

At this time the procedure is simpler and the mating of young queens is more effective.

Number of colonies

Should an artificial swarm be made from only one colony or two? One colony can certainly be successful. But it is always safer to use two, if you can you should, fifteen days later taking another swarm from the same two colonies. We thus describe both methods.

Day and time

Work on a fine day after a preceding fine day, and between 11 a.m. and 3 p.m., preferably at 11 a.m.

Choice of colonies

Always use the best colonies.

These are the ones with the largest number of bees. Big populations make the job easier. Furthermore, when using strong colonies you are making a useful selection without excessive effort.

Mated queen

Using a mated queen in artificial swarming is not only helpful, it is very helpful. You would be giving the swarm a head start.

Furthermore, if you have bought this queen from elsewhere you are bringing into your apiary new blood which always improves your stock. This improvement will be still greater if you give your swarm an Italian queen from a reliable source.

If you are uncertain of the reliability of the source of the queen you are buying, if you are not certain that the queen being supplied to you has not been raised according to so-called modern methods, artificial ones, do not buy a queen but rest content with those that your bees are raising themselves.

Procedure

To make an artificial swarm, be it with two colonies, with one colony, or with a mated queen, you proceed as described in the following figures.

Feeding

If the artificial swarm and the parent have not received honey in the comb and if the nectar flow has stopped for more than two days, it will be necessary to feed the swarm as well as the parent colony, and to do so more plentifully if they have to construct comb.

Swarming with one colony

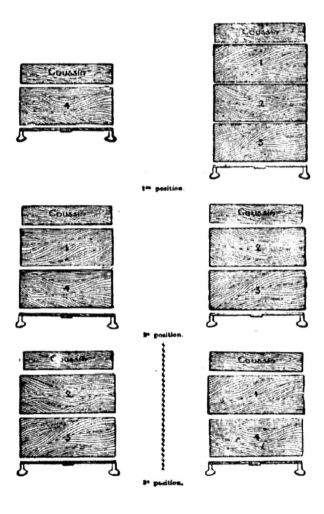

Swarming with one colony

1. Choose a good colony that deserves being increased. This is the colony of hive 1, 2, 3 (see figure on p.99).

2. Place beside hive 1, 2, 3, hive 4 comprising a floor, a hive-body box without bees, but ready to receive them, i.e. fitted with starter strips. Prepare a cloth and quilt to cover this hive.

3. Gently puff a little smoke into the entrance of hive 1, 2, 3 sufficient to calm the bees. Misusing the smoke causes the bees and the queen to move to the top of the hive. This prolongs the procedure.

4. When the bees are humming, open hive 1, 2, 3; lift the quilt and the cloth covering the top-bars. Smoke it vigorously.

Clean the tops of the top-bars and smoke vigorously and quickly between all the top-bars.

5. When the bulk of the bees of box No. 1 have gone down into box No. 2, remove box No. 1 and put it on the box of hive 4 after removing its quilt and cloth. Single bees are to be disregarded. But if you notice bees balling you should drive them down with smoking more copiously. The queen could be in these balls of bees. This happens especially when working in conditions that are too cold or after having smoked too much from below.

6. Cover hive 1, 4 with its cloth and quilt. Smoke hive-bodies 2 and 3; clean the top-bars of box 2 and cover the hive with its cloth and quilt, 2nd position.

7. Lift hive 2, 3 and carry it quite far away within the apiary, the further the better. However, a distance of two or three metres may suffice. But in this case it is good to put a few leafy branches between the two hives clearly to mark the separation, and force the bees to make a detour when going from hive to hive.

8. Put hive 1, 4 in place of hive 2, 3.

9. Reduce the entrance of the two hives to the winter state for a few days, until the bees' comings and goings are normal.

Comment

The queen has gone down into hive 2, 3 and will continue to lay.

If you do this at the beginning of the main nectar flow, and if, in autumn, you left only the necessary stores in box No. 1, there will certainly be brood with which the bees will raise a new queen.

Swarming with two colonies

1. Choose a good colony that deserves being increased. This is the colony of hive 1, 2, 3 (see figure, p. 101).

Choose another colony with a strong population. This is the colony of hive 5, 6, 7. Hive 1, 2, 3 and hive 5, 6, 7 should be at least between 2–3 metres apart. If not, place a few leafy branches between the two hives to clearly mark the separation and oblige the bees to make a detour to go from one hive to another.

2. Place beside hive 1, 2, 3 hive 4, comprising a floor, a hive-body box without bees, but ready to receive them, i.e. fitted with starter strips. Prepare a cloth and quilt to cover this hive.

3. Gently puff a little smoke into the entrance of hive 1, 2, 3 sufficient to calm the bees. Misusing the smoke causes the bees and the queen to move to the top of the hive. This prolongs the procedure.

4. When the bees are humming, open hive 1, 2, 3; lift the quilt and the cloth covering the top-bars. Smoke it vigorously.

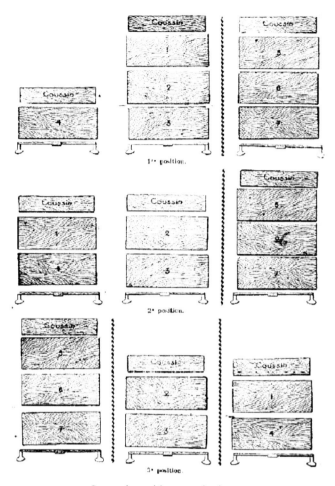

Swarming with two colonies

Clean the tops of the top-bars and smoke vigorously and quickly between all the top-bars.

5. When the bulk of the bees of box No. 1 have gone down into box No. 2, remove box No. 1 and put it on the box of hive 4 after removing its quilt and cloth. Single bees are to be disregarded. But if you notice bees balling you should drive them down with smoking more copiously. The queen could be in these balls of bees. This happens especially when working in conditions that are too cold or after having smoked too much from below.

6. Cover hive 1, 4 with its cloth and quilt. Smoke hive-bodies 2 and 3, clean the top-bars of box 2 and cover the hive with its cloth and quilt.

7. Lift hive 5, 6, 7 and carry it quite far off within the apiary, the further the better. However, a distance of two or three metres may suffice. But in this case it is good to put a few leafy branches between the two hives clearly to mark the separation, and force the bees to make a detour when going from hive to hive.

8. Put hive 1, 4 in place of hive 5, 6, 7.

9. Reduce the entrance of the two hives to the winter state for a few days, until the bees' comings and goings are normal.

Introducing queens

Advantages of fresh blood

In any breeding, introducing foreign blood is beneficial.

Therefore, from time to time introduce into your apiary a queen from elsewhere, preferably an Italian queen.

In an apiary of between 30 and 40 hives, where selection has been made for several years, new blood from elsewhere does not have the same advantage.

Moreover, we repeat that you gain nothing in buying queens unless you find a breeder who makes a good selection and does not practise modern breeding, i.e. artificial breeding.

Which colony to give the queen to

An introduced queen is best given to a poor colony. In this way you only destroy a bad queen. Or better still, you can give the queen to an artificial swarm, which is the easiest method because it does not necessitate finding and killing the existing queen. In addition it suffices for renewing the blood of your colonies.

Care of the queen

Once a queen has arrived, place her in a cool, dark place always enclosed in her travelling box. If her introduction has to be delayed, check the stores and supplement them as necessary using honey (a drop each day) by allowing it to flow through the mesh.

Preparation of the hive

If you are giving the queen to a swarm, you should introduce her into hive 1, 4. This hive is certainly queenless. You do not have to kill the queen.

When the hive is in its final position, gently smoke it through the entrance, open it and gently smoke the top and introduce the cage as described below.

If you are giving the queen to an already established colony proceed as follows:

Kill the queen of the colony to receive the young queen and destroy all the queen cells that may be present. If the colony has been queenless for some days, make sure that a queen has not hatched and destroy all the queen cells.

How to find the queen

To find the queen in a People's Hive proceed as follows:

Put all the occupied boxes of the hive on one side. On the hive floor place one or two empty boxes according to the strength of the colony. On top of the empty boxes place a queen excluder. On top of the queen excluder place all the boxes of the hive previously put to one side. Open the top box and smoke strongly and rapidly between the frames.

Clean the tops of the top-bars. When the bees have abandoned the top box, proceed in the same way with the other boxes. When the queen excluder is exposed the queen will be found amongst several drones. She is destroyed, or, if she is going to be used, placed in a cage.

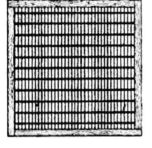

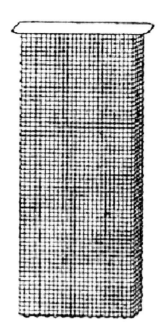

Queen excluder, made
of perforated zinc with
slots 4.2 mm wide

Queen introduction cage
(not to scale)

Queen cage

The queen cage, shown in the sketch, has given us full satisfaction. It is 10 mm wide, 45 mm long and 110 mm deep. The bottom is not closed. The top is closed with a piece of enamelled metal sheet or simply with a fold of the metal mesh. The mesh used for food safes is perfectly suitable.

Introducing the queen

Proceed immediately to introduction in the following manner: work preferably in fine weather and between 10 and 11 a.m. Take the box with the queen. Remove the box which has the address and which covers the grille.

Tear off the small card that closes the opening beside the stores and let the queen and the bees accompanying her run into your cage. Close this cage with a piece of comb.

Place this cage between the combs at the top of the top box forming the brood nest.

The combs should contain a little honey. The cage is not introduced until the honey has been uncapped. This allows the bees accompanying the queen to take some honey through the mesh of their cage.

Monitoring the queen

If the wax has not been removed in 24 hours, either the bees are not taking notice of the queen, or they are trying to get at her by attempting to get into her cage through the mesh:

In the first case, it is almost certain that there is a hatched or developing queen in the hive. She must be destroyed.

In the second case the queen has been accepted. It is therefore necessary to facilitate her release. Remove part of the wax. Get rid of any other obstruction, dead bees, etc. But do not remove all the wax. The bees will remove it and can only release the queen slowly as it suits them.

Put the releasing cage back amongst the combs.

Check it each day and remove any obstructions, but never the wax. A small opening will be sufficient.

Never release the queen.

When you have seen that the queen has been released, remove the releasing cage and a few days later you may check that the queen is laying.

Alternative swarming with two colonies

If a queen is not given to the queenless hive 1 and 4, in the case of swarming with one or two colonies, it will go on to produce a secondary swarm, possibly even a third. These swarms require a lot of monitoring. They often leave without our knowledge and are lost. The hive is emptied and reduced to a colony of no value. Here is how these swarms can be avoided:

1. Choose two strong colonies 1, 2, 3, 4 and 5, 6, 7, 8 (see figure above, first row). If these hives are not at least three metres apart, place a few leafy branches between the two hives to clearly mark the separation and obliges the bees to make a detour to go from one hive to another.

2. **1st operation:** Place beside hive 1, 2, 3, 4 a floor and a new hive-body box 9.

3. Gently puff a little smoke into the entrance of hive 1, 2, 3, 4; sufficient to calm the bees. Misusing the smoke causes the bees and the queen to move to the top of the hive. This prolongs the procedure.

4. When the bees are humming, open hive 1, 2, 3, 4; lift the quilt and the cloth covering the top-bars. Smoke it and clean the tops of the top-bars with the hive tool. Smoke it vigorously and quickly between all the top-bars.

5. When the bees in box 1 have gone down into box 2, put box 1 aside and cover it. Single bees are to be disregarded. But if you notice bees balling you should drive them down with smoking more copiously. The queen could be in these balls of bees. Do the same for box 2.

6. On hive 3, 4 place a new box 10; then cover it with cloth, quilt and roof. We now have a prime swarm with an old queen.

104

7. Lightly smoke hive 5, 6, 7, 8 through the entrance and move it at least three metres away. Otherwise screen it with leafy branches.

8. In place of hive 5, 6, 7, 8 arrange a new hive with floor, the new box 9 and the two boxes 2 and 1 put aside earlier; then cover with cloth, quilt and roof.

9. **2nd operation thirteen days after the 1st**: lightly smoke through the entrance of hive 1, 2, 9.

Open this hive; pass the hive-tool over the top-bars; move boxes 1 and 2 onto a box stand; place on box 9 a new box 11. On this box 11 replace boxes 2 and 1.

10. Smoke as before, to drive the bees down from box 1 into box 2, then put box 1 aside and cover it.

11. Drive the bees of box 2 down into boxes 11 and 9, then put box 2 aside and cover it.

12. On top of box 11, place a new box 12. Cover it with cloth, quilt and roof. We now have a secondary swarm with a young queen.

13. Smoke hive 5, 6, 7, 8, move it at least three metres away. Otherwise screen it from the others with a few leafy branches.

14. In the place of hive 5, 6, 7, 8, put a floor and new box 13, then on top of it boxes 2 and 1 put to one side earlier. Cover them all with a cloth, quilt and roof.

15. **3rd operation, 24 days after the first**: remove boxes 1, 2, 13 and use the bees to reinforce one, two or three weak colonies.

To do that, vigorously smoke the colonies to be dealt with. Remove one box from the hive that is to receive, place on it a queen excluder, on top of that place the box to be emptied, smoke it to drive the bees down, remove the box and, if a queen is found on the excluder, kill her and then remove the excluder and cover the hive again.

This is repeated for the two other boxes 2 and 13.

Bee diseases

Bees, like all living things, have their diseases.

We will not waste time describing them nor in indicating remedies. I will comment briefly, and for good reason.

Greater wax moth

Greater wax moth is recognised by the presence of large white grubs in the combs and of webs in between them. These grubs look very much like meat maggots; the webs, like spiders' webs.

In reality, wax moth is not a disease. It is not even an enemy of the bees. You find wax moth in all colonies, even the best. But the bees in these colonies do not allow the wax moth to develop.

In fact, wax moth only develops in weak colonies; but it does not cause weakness; it is simply the effect. The wax moth develops in these colonies because the bees, so few in number, are powerless to prevent its development.

If you follow my good advice closely, if you get rid of the weak colonies, either in spring or autumn, you will never have weak colonies invaded by wax moth.

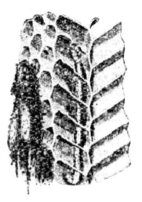

| Wax-moth larva | Cocoons and web of wax moth | Cocoons, web and tunnel of wax moth |

Foulbrood

Foulbrood is a deterioration of the brood at all stages of its development.

The cells holding the larvae, instead of being capped after the sixth day as is the rule, are pierced or uncapped.

Further, the dead larvae are transformed into a gluey mass which sticks to anything introduced into the cell, stretching out into a long thread when the thing is taken out.

Finally, the dead brood gives off a particular smell, rather like that of strong carpenters glue.

I do not go along with any curative treatment for foul brood. I do not know the value of the recommended treatments. But whatever the value may be, I guess that the game is not worth the candle.

Leave the use of treatments to scientists who want to pursue their studies on this point. We find ourselves unavoidably faced with a weak colony: let us destroy it like all weak colonies and replace it with a good swarm. We will thus gain time, money and honey.

But, in this case, it is best to destroy the bees with sulphur or any other means, to burn the combs and to really scorch the internal walls of the hive, or better still, to plunge them into hypochlorite solution (bleach).

The People's Hive is criticised for almost completely preventing the application of modern methods which are the future of our beekeeping. But it is my opinion that these modern methods are the death of beekeeping and that only the People's Hive and the skep will be able to save it. I emphasise the following facts.

The bee has survived for centuries in hives with fixed comb without suffering.

Things are no longer the same with the hive and modern methods. 'It is a certain fact', says Berlefech [*sic*, but could be referring to Berlepsch. *Tr.*], 'that the invasion by foulbrood in Germany dates from the same time as the framed hive. Before this time there was very little manipulation of hives, foulbrood was hardly known about as it was so rare; but, since then, it is as well known as it is frequent'.

Since this German's cry of warning, we notice in magazines, in manuals, at apicultural events that beekeepers are having to fight against foulbrood more and more. And they talk of fighting against this disease by creating a costly official bureaucracy, which will be a danger because it will carry the disease from a sick colony to a healthy one.

Let us not go against the laws of nature. Let us leave the germs to accomplish their mission, which is to get rid of what is useless, and let us give our bees the strength to fight against these microbes.

We see strong men untouched by tuberculosis germs, whereas weak men often give them favourable conditions for development. All in spite of having encountered tuberculosis germs in public places, on trams, carriages etc., in equal measure. Bees must be similar to men.

And the People's Hive and its method strengthens the bees through continual selection, by natural food, by eliminating all overworking of the bees and by the very fact that it protects the bees from foulbrood. Prevention is better than cure.

I am convinced that modern methods, which tend towards the intensive, lead quite simply to the degeneration of the bee. Since we have forced hens to lay more eggs, there are illnesses in the hen house which were formerly unknown. It will be the same in the hives.

The bee's enemies

The bee has many enemies, of very different kinds. These are: the owner himself, certain birds, some animals, even some plants.

The beekeeper

It does happen that the beekeeper does not know his job and treats the bees in a way contrary to their nature and needs.

The beekeeper must inform himself before setting up his hive. This manual, re-read frequently and properly understood, will suffice.

Birds

Many birds take bees in flight and eat them. These are often swallows and tits.

The green woodpecker works differently. He manages to destroy wooden hives and eat the honey in the comb. The blows from his beak are worse than the damage that he does to the structure of the hive. The noise agitates the bees which is very harmful in winter. Besides, the shock to the hive can lead to the separation from the group of a section of bees, causing them to fall to the floor, from where they will not get up if it is cold. The queen can be destroyed in this way. Bits of suspended glass and moving objects appear to deter green woodpeckers in sunny weather.

Animals

Toads will willingly eat bees that they find below the hive. These are lost bees, since they do not have the strength to fly again. In any event, the services that toads render besides are compensation for this rare bit of gourmandising.

Mice are harmful in the hives. They eat the wax and the honey, they destroy the combs to make their large, often very comfortable, nests. It is easy to prevent mice from entering the hives by reducing the metal entrances (mouse guards) in autumn and winter.

Plants

Bees fertilise many flowers and many flowers give the bees nectar and pollen. In contrast, there are some flowers where a visit from a bee destroys its freshness; there are also some which live off the bees that visit them, or which simply kill them.

The round-leaved sundew (*Drosera rotundifolia* L.) a small plant which can reach 20 cm, grows in peaty areas throughout France, and produces insignificant white flowers at the end of summer. A rosette of reddish leaves presses against the soil at the base of the flower stem which is covered with glandular hairs ending in a rounded head. These sort of tentacles have an extraordinary sensitivity, just as does the leaf itself. A weight of a hundredth of a milligram causes them to move, whereas a heavy downfall of rain has no effect on them.

At the moment when a tiny insect touches a tentacle it curls up in less than a minute: the neighbouring tentacles imitate the movement; a thick liquid secreted by the glands pours out over the insect, immobilises it, asphyxiates it, then digests it, leaving only the case and the wings.

If you put something inorganic on the surface of the leaf, the tentacles, unfolded in an instant, rapidly withdraw and the secretion is negligible. You cannot trick the sundew!

The butterworts *Pinguicula* and bladderworts *Urticularia* are considered to be carnivores plants, like the common butterwort (*Pinguicula vulgaris*) which grows in abundance in peaty grassland where it blooms in July. Its small flowers are white and violet; its leaves fleshy, of which the upper part is covered in glandular hairs, sessile or pedunculated, resembling little mushrooms. As soon as a gnat lands on this sticky and downy area, that is the end of it, the edges of the leaf curl round and plunge it into the darkness of the tomb, it completely disappears, except for the hard parts.

It is a particularity of the common butterwort that farmers use it to make the milk flow.
The flower of *Asclepia* uses glue to protect itself against insects. At the same time as secreting nectar, the object of their desire, it secretes a viscous liquid which holds them by the body or by the legs.

The harvest

Number of harvests

You can take honey out of the hives, when there is any, as often as you wish. But because it is always bad to open the hives, I advise you not to abuse this option.

In certain regions, the honey harvest is very different from one month to the next. If consumers will only accept certain honey to the exclusion of others, it is necessary to conform to their wishes and harvest the honeys separately.

But, in principle, I advise only one harvest. Even if there were certain hives with several boxes full of honey, though these boxes absorb some of the heat from the brood chamber, I still advise against harvesting. If there is one reason for harvesting, there are two for not doing so.

I have noticed almost everywhere that beekeepers do not leave enough honey for overwintering. They get a good harvest in July and they are short of honey later for their bees.

Some believe that the brood chamber has enough honey for overwintering. It is the same with beekeepers who do not do inspections. But what if they are mistaken? It is not unusual.

Others count on the second nectar flow. It is generally less than the first. And what if there is not enough?

Beekeepers hesitate to give the bees fine honey extracted with care. They give sugar. But sugar does not constitute normal food for the bee. It is constipating instead of being refreshing like honey. It can only cause harm to the bee, because in winter she has to stay for weeks without voiding herself at all.

Occasionally, beekeepers wait until spring has arrived before giving sugar syrup. Sugar is more harmful in spring: but feeding in spring is even more so. In effect, this feeding misleads the bees' instinct.

That is why I advise only having one harvest, at the end of August or beginning of September. At the same time as taking this honey harvest, you can sort out the winter stores. The two operations will be done as one and you will have all the necessary honey to hand.

But, you will say, the honey from the second nectar flow will be mixed with that from the first. The first will reduce the quality of the second.

In taking account of the fact that the second nectar flow is less abundant than the first, and that its quality is less different than one generally thinks, this mixing will change the overall quality very little.

And it is only from the marketing point of view that the second nectar flow would reduce the value of the first. From a health point of view, it can only improve it.

The health properties of honey are, in effect, multiplied by the number of flowers which have produced it. Now on the one hand, very white honey is only produced most of the time by sainfoin, a fodder plant without health properties, and, on the other hand, it is important to exploit the health properties of honey, because it is only in this way that it can fight sugar, its formidable rival.

Besides, in the People's Hive, the honey from the second harvest will be less mixed than in other hives with the other honey, since the combs are hardly raised and the boxes less capacious and the bees put the honey there working downwards according to the supply.

The honey at the end of the year will be found mainly above the brood, in the combs which must be left to the bees for the winter.

Time

The honey harvest must be at the end of August, or later, at the beginning of September.

At the end of August or the beginning of September, the bees will not gather any more honey. The flowers disappear or the temperature gets cold again preventing the rise of nectar.

This is the moment to inspect the hives and take account of the state of stores; reducing them if there is too much, making them up where they are not sufficient.

Winter stores

As stores you will need 12 kg in hives with fixed comb. Three decimetres squared of comb stocked with honey on both sides makes up 1 kg of honey. Furthermore, a comb of the fixed comb People's Hive contains six decimetres squared.

With this as given, it will be easy to work out what is lacking and what needs to be added; what there is too much of and what is to be taken.

Thirty-six decimetres squared of combs stocked with honey on both sides will be enough in the fixed-comb hive.

Insufficient stores put the bees' lives in danger or will necessitate spring feeding. But such feeding is always harmful and costly.

Too much in the way of stores is also harmful, because the bee does not winter on the cold and humid honey, but below it. As a result, the more honey there is, the more significant is the empty space to be heated above the bees. Besides, an excess of stores gets in the way of egg laying in spring.

Entrance

For the autumn and winter operations it is important to reduce the hive entrance by fitting the entrance piece with its wide entry (mouse guard). In the case of robbing, you would even arrange this door in a way which only allows one bee at a time to pass.

Procedure

To manage the honey harvest, proceed as shown in the following section, not forgetting that you must above all ensure the life of the bees by allowing sufficient winter stores.

In the following section, all possible situations have been envisaged. Thus at first sight, the operation appears complicated. We can summarise it as follows:

- Remove all the boxes which only contain honey.
- Stop at the first box where you come across some brood.
- Leave this box and the one immediately below it.
- Lift off the others if there are any.
- Assess the stores and make them up, if there is space. Place the two remaining boxes warm-way.

Comments

Stores: The dimensions of the boxes are such that a box which contains a somewhat small amount of brood can only contain a small amount of stores in addition, so small an amount that it is better not to reduce it, but to leave it as it is. For this reason, one operation in two is removed: you never reduce the stores contained in the two boxes left for overwintering, you supplement them only if necessary.

Toolbox: More than for any other beekeeping operation, the toolbox is needed at harvest time. You put even the smallest bits of wax and propolis in it, especially if they are wet with honey, in order to avoid robbing.

Honey under the brood: It must never happen that there is a permanent amount of honey under the brood.

That is why the honey combs from a box that you are obliged occasionally to put below will always be uncapped, so that the bees can take this honey and carry it to a better place.

The bottom box left for overwintering will occasionally contain a little honey which comes from the last supplies. There is no case for searching for it, nor to bother with it. The bees will eat it or carry it into the top box before it begins to hamper them.

Harvesting the honey

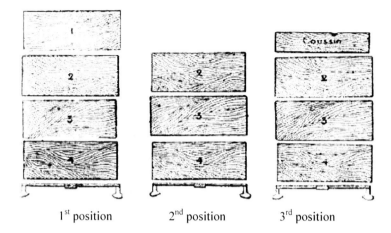

1ˢᵗ position   2ⁿᵈ position   3ʳᵈ position

1. The helper gently puffs a little smoke into the hive entrance and adjusts the entrance to its widest position. The beekeeper waits for the humming of the bees, then uncovers the hive.
2. The beekeeper rolls back the cloth covering the combs. The helper gently puffs a little smoke onto the uncovered top bars (first position, see diagram).
3. The helper continues gently using the smoker. The beekeeper passes the hive-tool over the top bars and the width of the side walls to remove the propolis.
4. The beekeeper takes the smoker and puffs plenty of smoke between the combs to make the bees go down from box number 1 into box number 2. If you leave the cloth on the box, the smoke which goes under the material is less likely to escape and the operation proceeds more quickly.
5. When the bees have gone down, using the hive-tool the beekeeper unsticks the first and second boxes, then lifts off number 1. He can turn it over to see it better. The helper gently puffs a little smoke on to the top bars of box number 2. If the beekeeper sees some brood at the bottom of the combs in box number 1, he counts the number of square decimetres of brood. Taking this figure from 48, he has the number of square decimetres of honey. Dividing this number by 3, he has the number of kilos of honey in the hive. It is better to err on the generous side. The beekeeper takes note of this number and replaces the box, covers it and goes on to another hive.

   If on the other hand, the beekeeper only sees honey in box number 1, he takes off that box and puts it in a safe place, covers it and goes on to another hive.
6. The beekeeper treats box number 2 in the same way as number 1. If he sees only honey, he lifts it off. If he sees a small amount of brood, he replaces it (second position, see diagram), then covers it (third position, see diagram) after having taken off what honey there is.

   And he carries on in this way. He takes off all the boxes which are absolutely full of honey. He stops as soon as he sees brood in the box.

Getting ready for winter

If you do not possess an extractor, you have to be able to borrow one, and then you have only to buy one single cage and two double. After the extraction you put all the combs back in the boxes without nailing them down for the bees in each hive to clean up overnight. Afterwards, you take out all the black combs for melting down. You fitted out the boxes which you are going to use with the white and lightly coloured combs. Those top bars have been nailed down as usual.

The helper smokes the hive through the entrance. The beekeeper uncovers the hive, lifts off the quilt but not the cloth which covers the comb. After the buzzing quietens, the beekeeper unsticks the top box from the one below, lifts it off and places it on a hive-body box stand.

The helper smokes the next box. The beekeeper passes the hive-tool over the top bars to remove the propolis from it. There is no need to make the bees go down. The beekeeper unsticks this box and lifts it up to inspect the comb.

First situation – If the combs are completely drawn, the beekeeper makes a note of it after having put it back in place on the floor. If there are still boxes on the floor, they must be lifted up before our box, that we have also been able to put on a hive-body box stand, is positioned on the floor.

The beekeeper returns to the first box put aside and puts it back in place.

Second situation – If, on the other hand, in the second box, the beekeeper notices that the combs are not completely drawn, he behaves in a different way according to whether he has or has not some drawn comb that he can use:

A: If he has drawn comb available, he puts the second box to one side and places the available drawn-comb box on the floor. On this box he places, as above, the first box which contains honey, brood and bees; but before covering it, he puts the undrawn box above to make any bees go down.

B: If he has no drawn comb available, he replaces the incomplete box on the floor and makes a note of the number of undrawn combs which it contains.

When all the hives have been inspected in this way, the beekeeper knows how much undrawn comb he lacks and how many boxes he can make up with unfinished ones. If necessary, he will get rid of some colonies by uniting two in order to have completely drawn boxes throughout.

To unite two colonies, using our excluder, he destroys one queen, the least good, the oldest, if he knows which, and uses plenty of smoke.

Often, at the time of these unitings, he finds some honey in the bottom box. It is best to uncap it with a knife or a fork.

He needs to follow this by feeding to make up the stores of all the hives which do not have 12 kg of honey. Our large feeder is particularly suitable for this.

Note particularly that a hive which produced a good harvest will need to be fed.

It can happen, though rarely, that the box to be taken off contains some brood. In that case you must wait for it to hatch.

Drawn comb

You must overwinter each hive with two boxes with completely drawn comb. The bees will overwinter better on drawn comb than in an empty space. But it is particularly in spring that the bees need these two drawn boxes, because they need them to put the brood in. If, in spring, the bees do not have these two drawn boxes to use, they will swarm just as if they had no space. In effect, they lack usable space, because there are not enough honey supplies for drawing comb.

Moreover, at this time, it would be extravagant to give the bees the necessary honey for the production of wax.

Therefore, you will unite some colonies if necessary, in order that all of them have two boxes with fully drawn comb. This destruction of colonies is being economical, in spite of appearances to the contrary. One good colony will produce more than two weak ones.

Destroying colonies

When comparing two colonies for uniting, you will notice that one is inferior to the other; it has less brood, less honey, fewer drawn combs. It is from this colony that you take the queen that you will destroy. Proceed as described in the section entitled 'Introducing queens'.

For uniting, proceed as follows: after giving them a strong dose of smoke, place the two boxes you want to keep on a floor, the one with the most honey on the top. Above these two boxes, put the boxes you want to get rid of, after having smoked them. Make the bees come down from the boxes that you are getting rid of by smoking them abundantly. Remove the now bee-less boxes. Cover the hive and smoke it well. The next day, if necessary, uncap the honey in the bottom box with a knife or a fork, and make up the stores if there are not enough.

In choosing which queen to keep, always give preference to the one which comes from a secondary or tertiary swarm (cast) as she will certainly be young.

Food

You need 12 kg of honey for a good overwintering in the People's Hive with fixed comb.

In carrying out the harvest, we left the first box where we found some brood. There might be between 12 kg and 14 kg of honey. All the colonies with such stores are in a good state for overwintering.

If a colony does not have this quantity of stores, say 12 kg minimum for the fixed-comb hive, you must give it to them immediately, and in one or several feeds.

For that, put an empty box below two boxes and proceed as described for extending the hive. In this empty box, put any container. In this container, you put broken comb or some honey syrup.

If you make up the stores with some honeycomb, it is better to break it up and sprinkle it with water.

If you make up the stores with honey syrup, it is important to put at least one third of water to two thirds of honey. In this case, you place on the surface a small board pierced with holes, or chopped straw or some small pieces of cork, so that the bees do not drown.

Sugar syrup can replace honey syrup. But you must not forget that sugar is not normal bee food and it will not give them such a good overwintering as honey syrup.

Do not forget, when feeding, to adjust the hive entrance piece in such a way that the bees can only use the small opening.

It is best to use our special feeder. See the section entitled 'Equipment'.

However, our large feeder is placed, by contrast, not on the floor, but on the top box.

Storing partly drawn boxes

You can store boxes with partly drawn comb and use them for extending hives in spring. To make sure they store well, you must burn the equivalent of half a sulphur candle below a stack of three boxes, sufficiently covered not to allow the sulphur smoke to escape through the top. You leave these boxes for twenty-four hours to absorb the smoke. Afterwards, you only have to protect these boxes against rats, which are very partial to wax.

The drawn boxes have little value with our method. In any case, it is important to only keep newly drawn comb. The completely drawn boxes could nevertheless be used to take in bees saved from suffocation (sulphuring). You then only have to give them some stores.

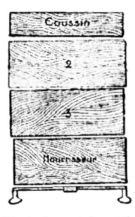

Position of feeder in empty box at the bottom

Extracting honey

The honey we have taken from the hives is in the extraction room but still in the cells of the comb that are capped with wax.

Comb honey

Comb honey may be sold as such, but account should be taken of the fact that transporting it is difficult, that by selling it this way the wax is lost, that the return of the hive boxes with the comb entails a cost, and that a new starter will have to be put on the top-bars.

This comb honey should not be confused with section honey, whose production I have not recommended because it goes against the bees and it is not profitable for the beekeeper.

If the beekeeper finds buyers for cut comb honey, which is less expensive than sections at harvest, he will only have to put these combs in a safe place to await sale.

Clear honey

Most commonly, the honey is separated from the wax before sale. This is called clear (runny) honey.

Clear honey is obtained in three ways: by letting it drain unaided or by assisting flow with heat or with the force of centrifugation.

Extraction by draining

This extraction is begun as soon as the combs have been brought to the extraction room. Using a knife, all the honeycombs are cut out in pieces leaving about 10 mm comb on the top-bars. Pieces of comb containing pollen are put aside as this pollen could discolour the honey. Bits of comb containing brood are likewise put aside if it happens that any are found.

All the other pieces of comb are put in a metal sieve of 4 mm mesh, in an ordinary colander or on a screen and crushed by hand or with a knife. The honey is collected in a ceramic or tinplate receptacle. Honey deteriorates in galvanised steel containers or those made of zinc or copper.

114

If this is done soon after the harvest, the honey is still warm and flows easily. If it cannot be done immediately after the harvest it should be done in a room that is sufficiently warm.

Honey obtained by this method is commonly called drained honey.

Heat extraction

When spontaneous flow has stopped there is still some honey in the fragments of wax. Furthermore, some thick and viscous honeys do not flow using the aforementioned procedure.

These comb fragments and those put aside because they contain pollen or brood are combined and exposed to the heat of the sun or an oven.

If this is done by the heat of the sun, all of it should be covered with a thick sheet of glass to trap the sun's radiation and stop bees robbing.

If it is done with the heat of an oven, it takes place some hours after removing the bread; or it is carried out in the oven of a kitchen cooker, in which case too great a heat should be avoided.

In both cases everything melts – honey and wax – and drips into the receiver under the sieve. Cooling separates the wax and the honey. The cappings of comb put in the extractor can be treated in the same way. Honey obtained by this method is of poorer quality.

It will often be more economical to give all the comb fragments to colonies low on stores. In this case our large feeder is most useful.

Extraction by centrifugal force

This extraction is done with a centrifugal extractor. It has the advantage of most complete removal of the honey and is the quickest and least laborious method.

Until now this method has only been used for frames from framed hives. Our cage arrangement allows comb to be extracted from fixed-comb hives. Furthermore, the combs are uncapped in these cages.

Before putting the combs in the extractor, the wax cappings covering the full cells are removed, as described in the following.

Uncapping knife

Uncapping is done with a special knife, or an ordinary one from the kitchen. It is important that the knife is clean and quite hot. It is useful to have several of them to use in succession, putting them in a vessel of hot water in between uses. The vessel can be usefully placed on a hotplate. The knife needs to be hot enough to pass easily under the cappings but not so hot as to melt them. The operator should use the knife like a saw, cutting only on the pull stroke and not on the push.

When the knife has passed right across the comb, the point of the knife is used to remove the cappings that are in the hollows of the comb.

Comment

Sometimes cells filled with pollen are found under the knife. Pollen is found in boxes of all hives. It is not poison as bees feed it to their young larvae. Consumers even like to find the flavour of pollen in their honey. However, to avoid discolouring the honey, I advise not mixing this pollen in and for this reason to pass the knife lightly and carefully under the cappings.

Heat required

So that the centrifugal extraction works quickly and efficiently, it is important that the combs are not allowed to cool. Otherwise they should be put in a warm place. It is best to extract in the afternoon the combs that have been taken from the hives in the morning.

Furthermore, the heat from the uncapping knife re-warms the honey and this facilitates its extraction.

Uncapping the comb

1. Turn the hive-body box containing fixed honeycomb upside down on some kind of support, two hive-bodies for example.

2. In order to detach the comb from the inside walls of the box, pass a knife down each side along the walls.

3. Turn the box the right way up.

4. Lift each end of the comb to disengage it from the rebate (Fig. A).

5. Take the top-bars with the comb (Fig. B) and place them in cage number 1, that has been prepared by placing it on an uncapping horse, so that the top-bar is at the top, to facilitate depositing the comb.

6. Rotate cage number 1 with the comb such that the top-bar is at the bottom in order to ease uncapping.

7. Uncap the exposed surface of the comb.

8. Place cage number 2 on cage number 1. Invert, remove cage number 1 and uncap the other surface of the comb.

9. Place cage number 3 on all, so that the comb is held between the two sheets of metal.

10. Place these two combined cages enclosing the comb in the extractor.

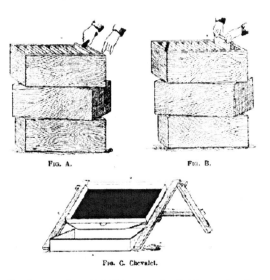

FIG. A.   FIG. B.

FIG. C. Chevalet.

A. Freeing top-bar; B. Lifting comb; C. Uncapping horse

Extracting honey with an extractor

All the cages in the extractor may have our cages placed in them. In any case, at least two should be put in four-cage extractors. Otherwise the extractor jumps during operation. Our cages should be placed in the extractor in such a way that the top of the comb is in front when the [tangential, *Tr.*] extractor rotates, or at the bottom when size demands, never at the back.

When the extractor's cages are loaded, it is rotated slowly, then rapidly. The honey escapes and hits the walls of the drum like rain. The cages are turned the other way round and the extractor rotated again, slowly at first then faster. The necessary number of turns of the crank is found by trial and error. It depends on the speed of rotation and the diameter of the extractor drum.

A distance covered of one kilometre in three minutes on each face gives a good result.

Honey leaving the comb reaches the extractor walls and runs down to the bottom. Before this honey reaches the height of the cages and thus impedes their movement, it is collected in a ripener.

Comment

Combs which are not too old or black can be saved, either to give to artificial swarms or to make up boxes with insufficient built comb. In which case extraction is carried out thus: spin them several times gently to empty one surface of the comb, turn the cages round, spin them several times gently to empty the other side of the comb, then spin more rapidly to achieve extraction of one face of the comb, turn the cages round and again spin rapidly to complete the extraction of the other surface of the comb.

Ripening

At the outlet of the extractor, the honey contains bubbles of air and various gases. It may also include pollen and capping debris.

To free honey from all these foreign bodies, it is left for several days in a receptacle called a ripener. These should be taller than they are wide. A barrel may be used for this if it is not made of oak. A strainer retains the larger impurities.

As a result of the different densities, the foreign material and the gas floats to the surface, and forms a scum that is removed before drawing off honey.

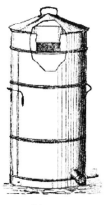

Ripener

If no more impurities are rising to the surface, the honey is drawn off before it crystallises.

Ripeners are fitted with a butterfly valve, or better still, a gate valve.

Crystallisation

The honey, a viscous liquid when it comes from the comb, solidifies and forms a compact mass of crystals varying in size. The honey is then said to have crystallised or granulated.

The temperature and the plant from which the honey came modifies *ad infinitum* the rate at which it crystallises and the size of the crystal grains.

A little old crystallised honey mixed in the bulk may haste granulation.

Storage of honey

Honey is hygroscopic. It can absorb up to 50% water. In absorbing water the honey liquefies. As a result it rapidly ferments and acquires a sour and unpleasant taste. To remove this sourness and stop fermentation it must be melted in a bain-marie.

The only way to avoid such difficulties is to store the honey in airtight containers and keep them in a cool place.

Containers for honey

Honey is kept in various receptacles, largely in barrels or drums made of wood or metal.

Pine or fir gives honey a resinous taste. Oak discolours it. Beech is very suitable.

Copper and zinc corrode on contact with honey. Tinplate is ideally suited to the purpose.

Therefore drums in tinplate with hermetic closures are to be preferred before all other receptacles.

Sale of honey

I am not in favour of big profits. But I hold that beekeeping, like any other occupation, should be honestly remunerated. All work deserves recompense.

In practice, therefore, how will the beekeeper set his price?

He will gladly accept the price resulting from the interplay of supply and demand.

To go against this principle, even with the powerful beekeeping associations, obliges our customers to eat foreign honeys, which are not all bad. That risks us losing our own honey which will not keep indefinitely.

When these prices are not sufficiently remunerative, we address ourselves to our elected representatives to ask them to set customs tariffs on foreign honey. If our request is justified, it will always end up by being listened to, especially if we have united to achieve strength. Above all, we produce cheaply.

The beekeeper must take account of the fact that wholesalers have the right to a profit, and the retailer has another profit.

The beekeeper may try to bypass these middlemen and himself be the wholesaler or the retailer or both. He will then have their profits. But he must not compete with them.

Beekeepers will still have need of middlemen for a long time to come. He cannot compete with them without working against himself. If he forces the middlemen to reduce their selling price, these same middlemen will lower their buying price the following year. The beekeeper's profit will therefore not last.

But there is the kind of middleman against whom beekeepers should start keen competition, and that is the retailer who profiteers and hinders honey consumption.

Now, honeys are not uniformly priced in commerce. How should a beekeeper categorise them?

In France, there are two well characterised sorts of honey: sainfoin honey, very white, with no marked taste, honey called 'Gâtinais'; and honey of multiple origin, more or less coloured, more or less aromatic, honey called 'Narbonne'. I mention, only to remind you, heather honey, honey called 'Landes'; and buckwheat honey, honey called 'Brittany'. These honeys of a red-brown colour and a sharp taste are not table honeys; they are only suitable for making gingerbread.

Now commercially honey called Gâtinais generally fetches a higher price. As beekeepers we should primarily place our honey in the category called Narbonne.

In selling honey the big problem is sugar, whose price is always lower and whose handling is infinitely easier. How can we make people appreciate the higher value of honey? By showing its superior health qualities compared with sugar.

But we are poorly armed to demonstrate the greater benefit to health of honey called Gâtinais. It certainly does not have the fault of being a chemical product, but neither does honey called Narbonne, which has more in its favour. Honey called Gâtinais has been foraged almost exclusively on sainfoin, a fodder plant without any health attributes. On the other hand, honey labelled Narbonne has been foraged from an indeterminate number of flowering plants, several of which are without doubt medicinal and beneficial.

A study done at the University of Wisconsin by Prof. Schuette showed that the greater the coloration of honey the richer it is in mineral substances, iron, copper and manganese. From this fact, dark honey is beneficial for preventing and curing anaemia due to poor nutrition.

Adulteration of honey

Honey has been adulterated for a long time. Herodotus, when he heard of the large quantity of honey produced in Lydia (Asia Minor), added that it was made largely by human industry. The Talmud also mentions honey adulteration by water and flour.

Current traders are neither more honest nor more stupid. It is at this point in time that calling it 'bee honey' no longer suffices to designate honey as natural, as people have now managed to get the bees themselves to adulterate honey by making them drink sugar syrup. Only the designation 'flower honey' will suffice.

To test for adulteration of honey, warm a sample in a bain-marie until it has become fully liquefied and stir it well with a wooden spoon, then:

1. Dissolve a teaspoonful of it in a Bordeaux wineglass of cold rainwater, stir vigorously and leave it to stand. An insoluble precipitate gradually forms if there has been an addition of plaster, ground brick, talc or chalk; i.e. any mineral substance;

2. Dissolve a teaspoonful of it in a Bordeaux wineglass of cold rainwater, leave it to stand, add three or four drops of tincture of iodine. It produces a beautiful violet coloration if starch has been added to the honey, intense blue if a thickener or flour has been added, brown if it is dextrin. On the other hand, the liquid is yellow in colour if the honey contains none of these substances;

3. Dissolve a teaspoonful of it in a Bordeaux wineglass of cold rainwater, and stir vigorously, beating it as one would eggs for an omelette; the liquid froths abundantly if the honey contains gelatine.

Beekeeping at a distance

With the People's Hive and its method, you can keep a hive some distance away.

First example

You can visit the hive twice a year: around Easter and in August/September.

In the spring, you do the spring inspection and enlarging the hive. On the whole, you should be generous with added boxes in order to reduce the number of natural swarms. There will occasionally be some nevertheless. The loss will be minimal by comparison with the honey harvest that you will get.

In August/September, you harvest the honey as described in the preceding sections.

Second example

You are only able to visit the hive once a year, in August/September. First you harvest the honey, then, as in the spring visit, you clean the floor if necessary, check the level of the hive and enlarge it straight away. Also, be generous with the boxes too, which it would be good to fix with lockslides.

The value of honey

Honey, saccharin and sugar

All sugars can be placed in three categories:

Saccharin: Saccharin is a coal tar derivative. It is a totally and exclusively chemical product. It has a sweetening power 300 times stronger than that of ordinary sugar. However, saccharin has no food value. It is found unaltered in the urine.

Sugar: Industrial sugar, sucrose or cane sugar is artificially extracted from sugar cane, from beet and even from other plants. In spite of its plant origin, sucrose cannot immediately be assimilated. In order to become so, it must be changed into glucose. This process is called inversion. It takes place naturally in our organism under the combined influence of saliva, gastric juices in the stomach and pancreatic juices in the intestine. If the digestive pathways are in a poor state, this takes place with some difficulty; in any event, it tires the human body. Outside the human body, in order to transform sucrose into glucose, we have to boil the sucrose with a very dilute acid for a certain length of time.

Honey: Natural plant juices and nectars contain glucose, fructose. Glucose is directly and immediately assimilated without the intervention of saliva, gastric or intestinal juices. This sugar imposes no special demands, and enters directly into the circulation to undertake its nutritive task. That is what explains why, far from being contraindicated, it is good for people who suffer with their stomach or who are prone to diarrhoea.

Whereas glucose and fructose do not exist in sufficient abundance where they are found, honey by contrast, contains glucose in considerable quantity. Honey from bees contains in effect from between 71% and 77% of invert sugar, glucose and fructose mixed in almost equal parts. Honey is the sugar of sugars, it is therefore foolishness to abandon honey in order to run after so many other sugary products, including saccharin.

Let us return to the advice of old Solomon: 'My son, eat thou honey, because it is good'.

Food and remedy

'In order to maintain health, you need two things: nourishment when you are healthy, and restoration to health when you are ill. Well, in honey you will find these two things: food and remedy'.

The plant realm occupies, in effect, an important place in cookery and pharmacology. Cookery could even be composed entirely of plants. Our ancestors ate little meat and lived for many years. Amongst certain religious orders, no flesh other than fish is ever eaten. And in our time, a school has been established to limit the use of animal products and increase the use of food from the plant world.

Medicine could also be entirely made from plants. An old adage says: *Medicina paucarum herbarum scientia* (medicine is the science of a small number of plants). Plant food is of sovereign healthiness and medication through plants very effective.

In a way, honey is a kind of abstract of the plant realm, as the bees go and gather it from an incalculable number of flowers of all sorts. And it is at the moment when the plant is preparing to reproduce, i.e. at the height of its vigour and strength, that the bee goes, carrying fertility to it and taking its rich nectar. So honey is a concentrated extract of the plant world, which borrows properties from plants. It is a herb tea of a thousand flowers.

Honey is better than sugar

Whereas water, nitrogenous compounds, mineral salts from food, satisfy the need for repair and building of the body tissues, sugar is the fuel for the human body, the main source of heat, of energy and muscular strength.

It is only in the special form of glucose that sugar can be absorbed by the organs.

Therefore it is not sugar chemically extracted from beet that we must absorb as a food which will give us strength. This artificial sugar is a precious condiment, convenient, indispensable; it is not at all a food. This sugar is after all only beet juice which, combined with its natural allies in beet has a certain beneficial usefulness, but is made harmful because it has been extracted from it by a chemical process.

Refined or beet sugar is extracted and purified using quicklime, carbonic acid, sulphur, beef blood, animal charcoal. Glucose, which accompanies or replaces it in confectionery, syrups or fruit preserves, is extracted from starch residues by means of sulphuric acid. Both products are bad: they are dead foods, irritating, devitalised and demineralised.

Artificial sugar spoils the teeth and dulls the appetite. It tires and overheats the stomach and intestines by using the invertase that they secrete, and which they already need in order to change the starches and fats from our food into glucose, thus giving them an abnormal amount of work which they are not intended for. It often happens that the sugar is partly rejected by the body without having been used, especially in weak, ill and diabetic individuals, of whom the digestive organs secrete scarcely enough invertase necessary for transforming sugar into glucose: from this situation arises a multiplicity of organ disorders.

Natural sugar, found in grapes, fruit and especially in honey, is the only one suitable for food because, naturally found in the desired form of glucose, this sugar is immediately assimilated and enters the blood at once, and as a result, without placing any strain on the digestive organs. In a word, honey is the steam that you put in the boiler; sugar is the cold water that has to be changed into steam.

Besides, honey is the sap of flowers, it is a sugar made by nature herself, the finest chemist.

This sugar, in a concentrated form ready for eating and storage, is offered to us in the honey gathered by the bees from the fragrant corolla of flowers.

In addition, if the honey is extracted mechanically by a well equipped beekeeper, it has no contact with the hands; it maintains an absolute purity and a cleanliness and as a result the delicacy of its smell and the richness of its properties.

Honey is a powerful food

According to recent research, 30 g honey has the same nutritive value as 21 g haricot beans; 31.33 g egg yolk; 35 g bread; 42 g lean pork; 48.20 g lean beef; 82.43 g skate; 64.43 g mackerel; 89.12 g potatoes; 122.50 g grapes; 123.50 g milk.

According to the same research, a small slice of bread and honey provides 169 calories, allowing 78 calories for the 30 g bread and 91 calories for the 30 g honey. Now a man doing a modest amount of work only needs 2500 calories a day. A calorie is a unit of heat, it is the amount of heat needed to raise the temperature of a kilo of water by one degree centigrade.

That is not to say that honey must constitute the whole of our nourishment, but should occupy a proper place in it. Because honey is a very rich food, as it is a sugar, and the most easily assimilated and as a result the most nourishing of sugars.

Besides, honey is food in a most concentrated form; it transforms itself almost completely into chyle, into blood. The proof of that is that the bee feeds itself with honey, during the long winter months, without voiding itself.

Honey is therefore the most appropriate food for our time of bodily indigence and organic degeneration. It is especially suitable for children, old people, people who are weak, convalescents, in particular for those who are anaemic.

Also honey should replace sugar, everywhere, especially in herbal teas, where besides it will add to their properties, since it comes from the flowers of the plants which make up the tea. In the morning, sugar your milk or your coffee with honey. Have it as a dessert after every meal. Spread on bread, on its own or mixed with butter, it makes the best snack for children and even for adults.

Should you want a good chocolate drink, melt some honey in a bain-marie and mix it with cocoa powder.

Honey is an excellent remedy

Natural honey, sap and quintessence of flowers, taken at the moment when the plant is at the height of its vigour and the flower is in all its beauty, is the most universal of remedies.

An eminent digestive by itself, honey also helps in the digestion of other foods. Its aromatic principles, its acids, stimulate the salivary glands, and besides honey does not use the gastric juices. This overabundance of saliva, of gastric juice, contributes to the digestion of other foods and carries along the accumulated residues from the stomach: that is why honey is digestive and somewhat laxative. Honey is thus especially suitable in cases of stomach ache, painful digestion, constipation.

Honey is also refreshing: it is recommended in cases of inflammation of the stomach and intestines, in kidney ailments and in bladder problems.

For insomnia: it calms the nerves and encourages sleep.

Many diabetics have benefited by using it.

Finally, honey contains iron and especially, formic acid, that formic acid so much recommended these days by medical experts in order to increase the activity and strength of the muscular system and to stave off fatigue.

Furthermore, this formic acid makes honey antiseptic: that is how it combats intestinal fermentations. Antiseptic, refreshing and calming, honey makes an excellent ointment for healing wounds, bruises, ulcers, spots and inflammations. For the same reason, honey is immensely useful in hoarseness, coughs, colds, influenza, bronchitis, tonsillitis, catarrh, asthma, and mouth ulcers in children.

We can therefore say that nectar is truly a beneficial juice, a panacea placed by the Creator in the chalice of the flower and reverently gathered by the bees.

To be thorough, we must say however, that the frequent use of honey would not be suitable either in the case of liver problems, because of its formic acid and because it encourages obesity, or in the case of a tendency to stroke, because honey is absorbed in the stomach and as a result rapidly, even violently.

What others say about honey

Sugar is an anti-physiological stimulant, a tiring food which profoundly exhausts after the brief over-stimulation that it produces.

It irritates the tissues, and the strength that it produces is only the expression of the attack that it makes on all our organs. It is an irritating and harmful chemical substance.

Honey, with its sugars already combined with mineral salts, with its active diastases, with its vitalised floral energies, is indeed a living and physiologically stimulating food whose use should be more widespread, because it is, so to speak, a hundred times more dynamogenic and nourishing than chemical sugar. Also it ought again to take up the important place it used to occupy in food before the discovery of chemical sugar.   *Dr Paul Carton*

Industrially produced sugar is strongly constipating and stimulating. It damages the stomach, destroys the teeth and often leads, even amongst the most robust individuals, to a marked glucosuria which can lead to true diabetes, because the digestive organs do not transform it and only partly assimilate it. We are not constituted to take advantage of it in this dead chemical form. The number of deaths caused by diabetes has, for this reason, quadrupled in the last thirty years and is ever increasing.

The true natural condensed sugar is honey. It should thus, contrary to our present habit, occupy first place in our diet.

The more the human being gets to know nature, the more he will want bees; and honey, the sugar of so many past generations, will again, we are convinced, be the preferred sugar of future generations because that is the truth of the matter.   *Dr Victor Arnulphy*

The aromatic principles and the acids in honey which give it its distinctive flavour and its scent, stimulate the salivary glands to produce more; digestion is thus made easier. But they also exert their antiseptic qualities on the stomach by counteracting gastric fermentation. In any event, the main effect of honey is exerted in the liver. Sugar, like honey, heads for the liver but it must, before that, undergo splitting into dextrose and levulose, whereas honey does not require any splitting, itself containing straight dextrose and levulose, substances which immediately go straight into the liver in order to pass

from there into the blood, so much so that honey is essentially digestive and hepatic, producing a
diuretic and laxative effect. *Dr Dubini*

There is another category of substances, much less important from the point of view of weight, but which impart a special character to honey. These are mineral substances.

Precise and detailed research studies have allowed us to set out the facts and to say that, thanks to the presence of these substances in natural honeys, they have become no longer just some food or other, with remarkable assimilability, but more, in certain situations, a strengthening food of the first order. Because these material substances are especially rich in phosphates and also in iron.
Alin Caillas

The miracle is the bee, from time immemorial, always making something which is at the same time agreeable to look at, to taste and to smell; something which is at the same time a dessert and a remedy, a food and a scent, a pleasure and a profit, a curiosity and a blessing. *Miguel Zamcoïs*

The bee alone knows how to extract the flower's most delightful property and at the same time to make of it something lasting, which does not vanish with the first puff of wind.

What is more entrancing is that through their delicate flower puree, bees do not allow us only to relate to the earth in a general way, but also in the most particular way. *Maurice Bouchor*

Most certainly, my fondness for bees is very much connected with what I like, like a bear – the delicious treasures that they give to us. It is probably thanks to this earthly ambrosia, that I have been able to reach, not without difficulty, my eighty-fourth year; and it is amongst the murmuring hives that I would like to sleep my last sleep. *Emile Blémont*

I taste the marvellous honey, slippery with round wax cells, and I seem to see the very fount of Poetry flowing and feeding me with its golden blood sweetened with loving flowers.
Jane Catulle-Mendes

Honey in foods

Honey should comprise part of the dessert at every meal.

Those who love it take honey instead of sugar in white coffee, tea, black coffee, and are very satisfied with it. It is true to say that, in hot drinks in general, to be agreeable, honey must have an acceptable taste.

You could spread a thin layer of honey on bread and butter, it is a delicious delicacy, found a lot in Switzerland. At least, after every meal, take a crust of bread – the honey is better with crust than crumb – eat it, covered in good honey, in three or four bites. Gourmets are warned that dessert wine is less good after honey: you must therefore have honey at the end. Before going to bed, take a spoonful of honey, or, if you prefer, a small glass of mead liqueur: your sleep will be most peaceful and your dreams sweetest.

Honey must take the place of sugar in prepared dishes, cakes and pastries but you must not heat it for more than fifteen minutes.

Toffees and honey sweets

Mix four teaspoons of grated [block] sugar, four of grated chocolate, four of butter or a half litre of cream, six teaspoons of honey, a little vanilla. Place in a copper basin on a high heat, stir with a wooden spoon, test in a glass of cold water (to check that the mixture has hardened), pour out onto a greased marble surface, mark out with a knife, allow to go cold, separate into pieces, place in a tin with layers of silver foil.

Honey nougat

Cook 1 kilo of good quality honey to small-crack stage, taking care to stir it from time to time to prevent it sticking; whisk four egg whites until stiff and fold them in with the honey. After this, reduce the heat and stir constantly with a wooden spatula to avoid boiling. Leave it on the heat until the honey, which the egg whites will have liquefied, has recovered the small-crack stage (which you test in a glass of cold water as above); having reached that stage mix in 1 kilo of almonds, blanched and dried in advance, either in the steriliser or in a low oven, so that they do not contain too much moisture. Next shape the mixture to a normal thickness, and before it goes cold cut the nougat in strips of the size you want. The almonds may be replaced with pistachios or filberts, or as is frequent, included.

Honey crunches

Take 125 g caster sugar; 65 g melted honey; 150 g good quality flour; 2 whole eggs.

Beat the sugar and the eggs together well. Little by little add the honey then the flour, beating all the time. Leave the resulting semi-liquid paste for half an hour.

Using a spoon, put small well-spaced heaps of the mixture on a greased griddle. After several minutes, when they are a golden colour, transfer them to a marble surface or a plate, where they will harden while cooling. (They keep well.)

Honey syrup

Boil 2 kg honey, 400 g water and 40 g chalk for two minutes. Add 50 g animal charcoal and an egg white mixed with water. Bring to the boil, remove from the heat and leave to cool for a quarter of an hour. Pass the warm syrup through a filter as many times as necessary to get it clear (to keep, it must reach 31° Baumé [density: 1.27 kg/l, *Tr.*]) then bottle.

Liqueur gilded with honey

Add enough water to 4 kg of honey to make 8 litres of mixture. Reduce to 4 litres by boiling, then mix (after cooling) with 3 litres of good quality pure alcohol in which 3 sticks of crystallised vanilla have been macerated for between 8 and 15 days. In this way you will get 7 litres of delicious liqueur.

Honey Curaçao

Steep 50 g orange peel, from which the bitter pith has been removed, in a litre of brandy for fifteen days. Add 600 g honey dissolved in 600 g water (or better, honey syrup). Add a pinch of cinnamon, one of mace and two cloves.

Aniseed honey

Steep 5 g aniseed for 8 days in a litre of spirits of between 18° and 20° proof. Mix with some honey syrup. Filter after cooling.

Strawberry cream

Infuse some strawberries in brandy for between two and three weeks, squeeze through a sieve, add some honey dissolved in water and leave to clear. Place in the sun to age. Follow the same procedure for creams of blackberry, cherry, raspberry etc.

Orange blossom cream

Steep 125 g orange blossoms in 2 litres of spirits of between 18° and 20° proof, for two or three hours; clarify, add 750 g honey dissolved in a half-litre of water, blend and strain.

Spice bread

Mix 500 g flour with 500 g honey. The flour you use can be wheat, rye, maize or buckwheat. Leave for several days. This mixture will keep for a very long time. When you are ready to cook, add 6 g potassium carbonate to taste.

Place the mixture in Pullman tins. Grease the moulds. Roll out the mixture to a thickness of about 2 cm. Cook over a low heat for about two or three hours. Turn the moulds two or three times so that they are cooked on all sides – after an hour they can be opened to check that they are cooking properly.

Honey pastilles

Melt 100 g sugar in 100 g honey over a low heat, then turn up the heat to crack point. Place spoonfuls, of the size that you want, on to a greased marble slab.

Honey macaroons

Mix 2 eggs with 200 g flour. Separately, mix 250 g honey and 125 g butter over a low heat. Stir the two mixtures together. Season to taste. Place drops of the mixture, about the width of a 1 franc piece, between three and four centimetres apart on a buttered baking tray. Cook in a low oven for five or six minutes. The macaroons will turn golden and spread. After they have cooled down they can easily be removed from the baking tray.

Honey in remedies

Thanks to its numerous properties, honey can be put to advantage in all sorts of ways, either internally or externally.

An Austrian surgeon, after experimenting, considered honey to be among the best healers, for the following reasons.

Ripe honey is treated by the bee in a way that allows it to keep almost indefinitely, she gives it the elements which guarantee its keeping qualities. For this reason and also because of its density and its sugars, no unhealthy germ is able to live in honey. Even living, dangerous germs, such as typhoid bacillus (which thrives in most food) perish if they are placed in honey.

Also, we may safely use honey for wound dressing, for burns and boils.

When we leave a pot of honey exposed to the air in a humid environment, we notice that the level of the honey steadily rises. It is because it is drawing water from the atmosphere.

In the same way, if we place bandages which have been coated in honey on a wound, the honey draws fluid from the tissues. This lymph carries with it the pus and poisons, and even attacks the microbe. The honey kills them through its antiseptic action.

In addition, honey contains two sorts of natural sugar, some mineral salts and the important vitamins. It is very probable that the cells and tissues of the wound absorb them when we apply the honey. If it is the case, then its curative power is even more understandable.

In order to effect a cure, wounds must be left undisturbed as much as possible. Honey softens and does not irritate the skin and, because of its consistency, sticks to the wound and softens everything. Not being greasy, it does not leave any excessive discharge, it does not dry out and the bandages do not stick.

Coughs, bronchitis, hoarseness

Take a coffee-spoon of warm honey every two hours throughout the day; one spoonful an hour before dinner and another in the evening before going to bed. If you mix the honey with a little goose grease, it will make the remedy more effective.

Mouth ulcers, thrush

Rub with honey to which you have added alum or borax. Or alternatively use rose honey made of honey and rose oil.

Influenza

Take some weak tea strongly flavoured with honey and a little rum and lemon.

Digestive problems

Honey, with its refreshing, gently laxative and purgative properties, prevents constipation and is very good for inflammation of the stomach, and even the bladder. According to Dr Guerin, there is no better treatment for gastrointestinal upsets, and he adds that honey would be the most important food for those with excitable constitutions.

Intestinal worms

Give children honey mixed with a little garlic.

Constipation

Take frequent doses of warm milk sweetened with honey.

Insomnia

Take two or three spoonfuls of honey before bed to calm the nerves.

Inflammation of the eyes

Dissolve some drops of pure, clear honey in a little warm water and bathe the eyes with drops of the liquid, four or five times daily, the last time just before going to bed. Some minutes afterwards, remove the secretions which leak out from under the eyelids, without however, cleaning the eyes themselves.

Ulcers, abscesses

Use an ointment made of heated honey kneaded into rye flour or boiled onions.

Burns

Make compresses of honey or honey water.

Cracked skin, scurf

Make lotions of honey diluted with water; or late evening, rub the hands with honey and wear gloves. Use honey soap.

Honey soap

Knead 50 g. of good white soap (grated) with 130 g. honey, 16 g. cream of tartar and 70 g. orange flower water.

Skin inflammations

Make lotions of honey diluted in water.

Shaving rash

Make lotions of honey water or rub with a little honey before wiping clean.

Skin care

The much vaunted cosmetics and soaps do not surpass honey water for giving skin whiteness and softness.

Honey does not burn the skin as glycerine does. It does not block pores with impurities as do fats. But glycerine and fats occur in all commercial preparations.

To give skin whiteness and softness, nothing surpasses the following recipe. It has only one fault and that is it is so easy. Mix liquid honey and cornflour to form a thick paste. Before washing yourself, spread this paste on the skin. Rub for as long as possible, rinse off and wash.

Cod liver oil

Cod liver oil can be replaced by honey-butter comprising two parts fresh butter and one part honey beaten together. This cream with a white glaze, fresh tasting with a hint of Sauternes, is more easily accepted by children.

Whitlow

To heal whitlows or suppurating wounds, take one egg yolk, an equal quantity of honey, a teaspoonful of camphorated alcohol and a soup-spoonful of really fresh turpentine; mix well and make into a paste with a clear consistency. Spread a thin layer on the wound and keep cool. This paste has an amazing power to draw and remove pus; healing is very quick.

Mead

Comment

Mead is an alcoholic drink made by fermenting honey.

I do not see a future for mead. It is more expensive than wine and often not as good. However, it may have its place amongst those who like it and all beekeepers.

Making mead is a difficult procedure. To understand the problems it is important, to know what fermentation is.

Those who do not want to specialise in mead production and who want a good product without the risk of excessive expense, I advise to entrust their honey to a specialist in honey fermentation, who will give them in return a good quality and pleasant mead.

Fermentation

Fermentation is the growth and multiplication of a microbe, an infinitely small organism, in water, which is its medium just as air is ours, under the influence of appropriate nourishment, sugar. The alcohol contained in the water after the fermentation is like the excrement of these microbes.

There are many kinds of microbes that can carry out this fermentation. They differ in vigour; their products are not all the same.

It is therefore important to eliminate bad microbes and use those that give good results, vigorous enough to resist the bad microbes. It is important to eliminate everything that holds up the growth of good microbes and on the other hand to give them everything that will favour their growth.

It is thus necessary to dispense with making sweet mead. Excess sugar retards fermentation. Alcohol production also retards fermentation the more the alcohol concentration approaches 15 degrees. The microbes are inhibited by sugar and alcohol just as if we were to be plunged in excrement or milk, for example, which is nevertheless one of the best foods for us. However, they will be less inhibited than us because these infinitely small organisms have greater resistance.

Now, a slow fermentation allows foreign microbes to appear. These have a lower value and give us an inferior product or reduce the value of the product in the long term.

Making sparkling mead should also be avoided. Making this requires a knack that is possessed by specialists.

Degree

Mead should be made to 8–10° alcohol. This concentration is sufficient to assure that the liquid keeps well. Otherwise a mead does not contain enough sugar and will never acquire enough alcohol to inhibit fermentation.

Temperature

The best temperature is from 20–25°C. Above and below this temperature, fermentation slows down.

Traditional method

In this method, pollen was used to ferment mead. It should be abandoned as it has never given French meads that taste good and are pleasant to drink.

Artificial method

In this method the honey only provides the sugar and the alcohol. The fermentation is artificial. Because of the loss during production, 24 grammes of honey is used per litre and per degree, i.e. 2.4 kg per degree in 100 litres; 24 kg per 100 litres of mead of 10 degrees. Boil the honey in a tinned or enamel cauldron with an equal weight of water. Remove scum. When the syrup is clear, add 6 grammes of nutrient salts *Le Clair* and 60 grammes of ammonium phosphate. Pour into a scrupulously clean cask of 100 litres capacity. Fill the cask to within 10 centimetres of the rim with pure water or preferably boiled water.

When the liquid's temperature has fallen to 20–25°, pour in 120 grammes of tartaric acid dissolved in a little hot water, 10 grammes of tannin in water, then 500 grammes of yeast of any of the following varieties: Champagne, Sauternes, Chablis. Yeast from other sources does not give the same results.

Stir vigorously and insert a fermentation lock. After 15-20 days, rack off into a sulphured cask. If the liquid is cloudy, clear it with 2–3 grammes of isinglass. It may be bottled a month later.

Natural method

In this method some fruit provides part of the sugar and alcohol, all the yeast, tannin and salts. In our view this is the best method, especially if the fruit provides at least a third of the sugar.

Here is a recipe that has given us good results. The fruit provides three tenths of the sugar, the honey seven tenths.

Boil 17 kg of honey in a tinned or enamel cauldron with an equal weight of water. Remove the scum. When the syrup is clear, add 60 grammes of tartaric acid. Transfer to a scrupulously clean 100-litre cask. Crush in a tub any of the following: 35 kg grapes; 45 kg cherries; 60 kg plums; 75 kg gooseberries; 75 kg strawberries; 80 kg currants; 100 kg blackberries. Add to the cask when its contents are at a temperature of 20-25°. Fill the cask with fresh, or preferably boiled, water. The fruit should of course be of high quality and thoroughly ripe. They can be mixed to advantage, keeping the proportions given. If one is using two types of fruit take, for example, 30 kg plums and 50 kg blackberries. If using three types of fruit, take, for example, 20 kg plums, 33 kg blackberries and 12 kg grapes.

A fermentation lock is placed on the cask. The cask is rolled from time to time to disperse the crust. When fermentation ceases the liquid is racked off into a sulphured cask and cleared as usual. Finally, the mead is bottled when it has properly cleared.

Wax

After the honey has been extracted, the wax cappings and comb fragments remain. After driving bees from a skep and extracting its honey we are also left with the remains of dry and empty comb.

Two forms of wax are available for rendering: dry wax (*cire en branches*) and wet wax (*cire grasse*).

To render wax for further use, it has to be separated from its impurities: pollen; larval corpses, cocoons of pupae, dust.

Comments

1. Various methods are used for purifying wax involving melting either by solar heating or in an oven or with hot water. These three methods are based on the fact that beeswax melts at a temperature of 62–64° and that in melting it separates spontaneously from its impurities because it is less dense, i.e. about 0.965 kg/l.;

2. The closer the melting temperature is to 64° the better the quality of the wax.

3. Cast iron and un-tinned steel gives wax a brown colour. There are also certain waters rich in iron. Tinned steel can be used.

Melting by solar heating

Solar wax extractors for melting wax this way are commercially available. They are based on the same principle as the gardener's cold frame.

These extractors may reach a temperature of 88°. This temperature is attained more readily if the inside is painted black, by using thick glass, by adding a second sheet of glass above the first and by keeping the extractor facing the sun.

This method of melting is economical and does not have the difficulties of the others. Moreover it gives an excellent product. But it largely suits cappings and really clean dry comb (*cire en branches*). The impurities in the other methods absorb some of the melted wax. I do not know if this loss of wax is more than the saving in time and fuel. I doubt it. I have high regard for the solar extractor. Unfortunately it can only be used in summer.

Melting in an oven

This method is also economical, but it often happens that the wax burns, acquires a brown colour and an unpleasant smell.

In any case, here is how to proceed with melting this way. The combs are broken into small pieces and placed in a metal mesh strainer or in an ordinary colander. Underneath is placed a receptacle of appropriate size containing water to a depth of four or five centimetres. All are placed in a bread oven after the bread has been removed or in the oven of a kitchen cooker. When the wax has melted, it is left to cool very slowly and without disturbing the receptacle containing the wax.

Melting with hot water

Melting this way is quicker and gives a good product. It suits all types of wax and any amount.

Three days before melting, the combs are broken into small pieces and immersed in water. After these three days the melting is carried out as follows.

The procedure can be carried out on a kitchen cooker, but precautions should be taken to ensure that no wax falls on the cooker as it is very inflammable.

A bowl is placed on the cooler part of the cooker containing four or five centimetres of water on top of which is placed a mesh sieve or an ordinary colander.

Preparations are made for a plentiful supply of boiling water in a boiler or otherwise.

Then a sufficiently large receptacle is taken, a washtub for example, and filled with water to one-third full. This water is brought to the boil. The crude wax that has been soaking in advance is tipped into this water. This tub is filled to no more than two-thirds so that if the water boils, the wax does not spill on the cooker. Furthermore, such boiling should be avoided so as to keep the wax at its best. It is useful to have cold water to hand to pour into the tub, in case one is caught by it boiling.

The wax once tipped into the tub is stirred until it has completely melted. Then it is immediately removed with a large spoon to put it in the colander or sieve prepared on one side. Boiling water is poured into it until no more wax comes out.

The residue left in the colander or sieve is discarded and the procedure repeated.

When this is finished, or the bowl containing the wax is full, the bowl is placed in as warm a place as possible. In any case, it is surrounded by insulation, sawdust, etc. so as to slow its cooling. The remaining impurities sink to the bottom. The slower the cooling, the cleaner the wax.

Alternative method

Put all wax debris in a strong cloth (old sack). Tie it firmly to form a kind of ball. Take your household washtub, cover the bottom with some twigs to stop the ball contacting the bottom of the tub. Put the ball in the tub and fill with water so that the ball is covered to a depth of 10 centimetres. A stone or a weight will keep the wax under water. When the water is sufficiently hot, the wax rises to the surface of the water. Squeeze the ball from time to time with a stick. When no more wax comes out of the ball, remove the tub from the heat and allow it to cool slowly.

Purification of wax

During cooling, the small impurities fall to the bottom of the bowl. After the wax has set they form a layer of varying thickness under the block (*pied de cire*).

This layer is scraped off. The wax is then re-melted as many times as necessary to obtain the desired purity. Each time, the sediment layer is scraped off.

The re-melting is preferably done in a bain-marie to avoid charring, and in a bowl containing a few centimetres of water.

Comb that is mouldy and partly eaten by wax moth only ever gives at first attempt a poor quality wax, as setting, even at the slowest rate, is unable to purify it. In this case it is necessary to make the liquid really adhesive by adding substances that trap the impurities and force them to be deposited.

The best adhesive agent is furnished by a mixture of half a litre of sulphuric acid added to two litres of water. To avoid dangerous spitting, the acid is added slowly to the water, never the other way round. This is the amount for about 100 kg melted wax. When the wax is very dark with excessive impurities, three quarters of a litre of sulphuric acid are added for 100 kg wax. Take care not to start a fire.

Sulphuric acid can be replaced with alcohol. Alum also shows the same clearing properties. In this case, one gramme of alum is added per litre.

A small amount of gelatine may be added to the melted wax.

Moulds for wax

Wax moulds are sized according to the tastes and needs of each person. They are greased with oil and warmed before pouring in the wax.

A wax block should be slightly bulging at the top. If the wax is poured too cold the bulge is more pronounced and there are parallel lines on the sides of the block. If the wax is poured too hot the top surface is furrowed or covered with deep cracks. It may be found helpful to add a small amount of hot water to the bottom of the moulds.

Cleaning moulds and bowls

To clean the moulds and bowls used in rendering wax, they are rubbed with sawdust while they are still hot. They can also be boiled in washing soda containing sawdust.

Colour of wax

Purified wax varies in colour from pale yellow to yellow-brown. It is thought that this colour is given to wax by the pollen that the bees consume while they are making the wax.

Adulteration of wax

As beeswax fetches a very high price and the pure substances to adulterate it are very cheap, it often happens that the wax is adulterated. Without making recourse to difficult and costly chemical analysis, it is possible by the following methods to see if the wax is pure.

Melt the suspect wax. If it is pure, it melts between 62 and 64°. If it melts one degree lower, or only one degree higher it is not pure.

Dissolve the wax in turpentine. Pure wax remains transparent, dissolves completely and causes no deposit. If there is a deposit, dissolution is incomplete or the solution is turbid, the wax is adulterated.

Profit from wax

Beekeepers who use frames produce little wax. Those who use fixed comb produce a lot especially if they practise suffocation (sulphuring) of the bees.

Uncapping comb from frame beekeeping yields a quantity of wax equivalent to one or two percent of the honey extracted.

Skeps yield wax in proportion to their capacity.

A hive of 30 litres contains 10 litres or cubic decimetres of space between the combs and 20 cubic decimetres of comb. Now, a square decimetre of comb contains 11 grammes of wax. But by ordinary methods only 6 or 7 grammes are extracted. A skep of 30 litres will therefore yield 500 to 600 grammes of wax. The remainder of the wax, 300 to 400 grammes, stays in the residues which certain companies may turn to account using suitable solvents.

Note that the weight is no guide to the value of the wax. Old, thick, black combs contain as much wax as others, but not more. Their greater weight is due to the impurities that have accumulated in them and which even impede the extraction of the wax by absorbing it.

Polishing wax

Yellow wax, 400 g.; rosin, 100 g.; turpentine, 100 g.; animal charcoal, 150 g.

Melt the wax in a bain-marie. When it has melted, in a room without a fire and by day, add drop by drop the resin that you have previously dissolved in turpentine, then add the animal charcoal and stir until it has completely cooled.

The less charcoal added the lighter the colour of the resulting polish.

Encaustication (painting) of floorboards

Here is an excellent recipe.

Yellow wax, 1 kg, potash dissolved in a little water (half a litre).

After having boiled these two substances in two litres of water for half an hour add 125 g. yellow ochre. Remove from the heat, stir the mixture vigorously until it becomes lukewarm. Spread the first coat on the wooden flooring that has been well cleaned in advance and allowed to dry. When this coat is dry give it a second coat.

Propolis

About propolis

Propolis, a rampart or barricade for defending the city, has been known from the time of Aristotle.

Propolis contains 76.27% wax, 22.15% resin and 1.58% water and volatile oils.

Propolis is a very sticky substance, malleable when it is warm, brittle and hard when it is cold.

It is a resinous substance which the bees collect from the buds of pine, fir, poplar, sweet chestnut, willow, etc.

Bees use propolis to erect defensive walls and to embalm small animals that have entered the hive and which the bees cannot otherwise remove, for example mice, lizards, cockchafers, snails, etc.

If the flight hole is large, to protect themselves from hawk-moths and various predators, bees often build two or three rows of pillars out of propolis and wax across it. These staggered pillars form a narrow resinous entrance allowing only bees to pass.

Dealing with propolis

Propolis placed in the voids of the People's Hive with fixed combs causes no inconvenience. Moreover, there is little of it.

In spring, when it is time to enlarge the entrance to the hive, propolis is removed from around it. But the entrance will certainly not have been reduced if it has been fitted with a metal entrance piece (mouse guard).

As regards the propolis that is always found on the tops of the top-bars, it is removed each time the top-bars are exposed, so as to ease replacement of the boxes by sliding them horizontally.

After preparing the hive for winter there is no reason to open the hive. In any case, at this time it would be harmful to remove propolis. The galleries made with it are used by the bees in winter and facilitate their movement. This is all the more reason to carry out the honey harvest and preparation for winter early enough.

To minimise propolisation of wood, cloths and tools, it is very useful to smear them with Vaseline or oil.

Wood and tools coated with propolis are cleaned with alcohol, ammonia, petrol or turpentine.

Purification of propolis

Expose it to cold to harden it. Then grind it up. Cover it with boiling water. The propolis melts along with the wax it contains. After re-cooling you will have a cake of propolis at the bottom of the bowl and on the surface of the water a crust of wax.

Use of propolis

Propolis can be used to make varnish. Grind some purified propolis. Dissolve it to saturation in a bowl of alcohol. It will dissolve. You will have a varnish that can be coloured with pigments. This varnish spreads with a brush and dries quickly. The varnish is made a lot shinier if it is exposed to gentle heat in an oven.

The varnish can be used to paint hives, especially the top of the roof. Inside the hive it may be pleasant for the bees and could attract swarms.

In any case, the varnish could replace grafting compound, sealing wax, etc. It could also be used for sealing leaks in watering-cans; filling joints in joinery and cracks in barrels, and for preventing rusting of stove-pipes.

In its natural state, propolis can be used in the smoker and can also be burnt on live coals for purifying and perfuming the air of rooms.

Winter feeding

Comments

Beekeepers should not need to feed their bees in winter. Making up the stores, if they were insufficient, should have been done in the autumn, at honey harvest time, or at the time of preparing for winter.

However, occasionally one may lack time or inclination. Here is a means of making good such a delay.

Feeding is more harmful in winter than in spring. It is therefore better not to feed in winter unless the colonies are absolutely in need of it. Supplementing the feed will be done in spring, i.e. in March or April.

Fondant

I advise against using fondant or candy. It is difficult to make and it often happens that you end up with caramel without intending so, and this burnt sugar cannot be given to bees.

Furthermore, commercial candy is always made of sugar which is not suitable for bees, least of all in winter.

However we offer the following recipe for candy for bees:

Put 3 kg crystallised sugar in a preserving pan, add a litre of boiling water to facilitate rapid dissolution while stirring the contents on the heat. Bring to the boil on a hot flame for between 15 and 20 minutes so as to reach a temperature of about 120°C, continuously stirring. While it is boiling add 3 grammes of cream of tartar and, near the end of cooking, 0–500 grammes of honey.

Allow to cool to about 35–40°. Take a good spatula and stir vigorously.

A chemical phenomenon takes place more or less spontaneously transforming the syrup into a white paste which can be moulded according to requirements. This candy is guaranteed to look white and like a fondant sweetmeat.

Jam-jar

One may always make use of a jam-jar covered with cloth and inverted on the combs. But at this time, it is necessary to put pure honey in the pot with some water added: honey two thirds, water one third (by weight).

For this preferably use a jar of clear glass so that you can see when it is empty, without lifting it. Fill the jar with warm syrup, cover with a cloth of not too close a weave and tie it with string. Invert the pot on a square of metal mesh in the middle of the cloth covering the top-bars after cutting out of it a square smaller than the mesh. Put an empty hive-body box on the hive and fill it with rags to conserve heat round the jam-jar. Cover the hive with its quilt and roof.

Sugar paste

Sugar paste can also be used. We draw your attention to the fact that granulated or caster sugars are not suitable for making this paste.

They have to be ground to a flour, or icing sugar should be used.

Icing sugar is best for making this paste. If none is available, the sugar one has in stock is reduced to powder.

To make the paste melt 750 g honey without adding water. Add sugar bit by bit, while working the mixture. Stop when the honey will not absorb any more sugar, 750 grammes of honey easily absorb 1 kg sugar.

Sugar paste is better than fondant but not better than honey.

Using sugar paste

The paste is placed in a thin cloth like a poultice then deposited on the top-bars under the cover-cloth.

In any case it is important to work quickly to minimise heat loss from the brood chamber and carefully to cover the brood chamber to keep it at the right temperature. Our quilt, if well filled and packed, is sufficient for this.

Beekeeping in winter

Cleaning the hive-body boxes

After having recovered the boxes given to the bees to clean out the honey, they are cleaned as soon as possible and the propolis and wax sticking to them removed.

We prefer to remove all the comb leaving only 5 mm which serves as a starter.

However, very straight, white comb can be retained.

In any case, this work should be done early because the wax should be melted as soon as possible and because in winter comb cannot be handled without damaging it.

A sulphur candle is burnt under the combs to protect them from wax moths.

Storage of hive-body boxes

The boxes are stored away from damp and rodents. Rodents are very fond of wax and even of wood to which some wax or propolis adheres.

Inspection of equipment

In winter, beekeepers can repair old equipment that is not occupied by bees and make new equipment or place orders so as to receive equipment in time.

Leisure time

Bad weather and long evenings give leisure time. Beekeepers can benefit from this by rereading books and journals on beekeeping. A second read enables one to understand what was not understood the first time, and appreciate what at first was judged to be of no value.

Beekeepers will also benefit from leisure time to note the difficulties they had and the observations they made and communicate them to the editor of their beekeeping journal. If everyone were to do the same, advances in beekeeping would be faster.

Moving hives

When there is a need to change the site of a hive it can be done in winter after the bees have not been out for 10-15 days, without any precaution other than ensuring that the hives are not jolted.

I do not like moving hives in winter. The slightest knock may detach the bees, even the queen, and put their lives at risk. I prefer to move hives in the warmer months, from the beginning of March, and proceeding as described in the following.

If it involves a move of at least three kilometres, one must first deal with the ventilation of the hive, because it often happens that the bees die of suffocation during the journey. To ventilate the hive it is covered by a metal mesh without anything else during the journey. The entrance is closed in the evening with a metal mesh and the move made as quickly as possible, taking care to orientate the combs parallel to the direction of travel and to avoid shocks so as not to break the comb.

If it is a small distance proceed as follows: the first day, in the evening, put all the hives in disorder by turning them in different directions without moving them from their existing sites. On the second day, in the evening, change the disorder and move all the hives three metres, and repeat this procedure, always working in the evenings, modifying the disorder and tripling the move each day.

Of course, it is important always to avoid shocks.

In summer, to move a hive less than three kilometres, people advise putting it in a dark cellar for three days before moving it to its final position.

Leaving bees in peace

You will avoid giving the hives even the slightest jolt. This applies in winter as much to moves, which are preferably done in March or April, as to repairs, which should be done before or after winter. Any disturbance of the hive causes the bees to hum and makes them consume more honey.

In winter, opening the hive is avoided for whatever reason. It causes chilling and consumption of honey which the bees turn into heat in such circumstances.

For this consumption of honey is a loss to the beekeeper. Above all it constitutes a harmful over exertion of the bees. The summer generations of bees work 24 hours a day when circumstances permit it.

The winter generation has to repair the over exertion of previous generations by a total rest so as to avoid degeneration of the colony. Let us respect the laws of nature. *Et vidit Deus quod esset bonum* (Gen.). And peace be with the bees in winter.

Our method is economical

We can now see that the People's Hive is as economical in the method applied to it as in the construction of it we have spoken about earlier.

It is economical because it eliminates wax foundation, because it saves a lot of time, and because it looks after the health of the bees.

Elimination of wax foundation

Embossed wax foundation is expensive. One also has to consider the time needed to put it in place.

The beekeeper has to place in each frame of his hives four or five hooks, then join these hooks with a steel wire. All this has to be very small, of course, and yet it must hold fast. To fix a sheet of wax in the frame the beekeeper has to heat a spur embedding tool sufficiently to immerse the steel wire in the wax, but not so much that it cuts the wax sheet. When the beekeeper cuts the wax sheet, which happens to the most practised, he throws the sheet in the melter and recommences the procedure with another. If beekeepers are concerned about the vigour of their bees they would renew all the wax of their hives every three years, i.e. one third each year.

It is clear that this work incurs considerable expense and above all takes up valuable time. But we should try to reduce the cost of production of honey. What should be done? Purely and simply dispense with wax foundation.

But beekeepers insist that using wax foundation is economical and guarantees straightness of the combs and reduces drones.

I know well that when the bees are made to build comb out of season, they use a considerable amount of honey for it. Even if we give the bees wax foundation the amount will still be too big to be feasible in a profitable apiary. Wax foundation is only a feeble initial contribution to the construction of combs and in addition the bees often modify it before using it. Whether one does or does not use wax foundation, there is only one time when we can get the bees to make comb and that is at the nectar flow. For, during the nectar flow, the bees exhaust themselves so much that they must consume more and they are so active that they cannot but perspire. And bee sweat is wax that they can use in the construction of comb, which is lost if they do not have comb to construct.

Thus the worker perspires without wishing to during her hard work of harvesting under the hottest sun of the year. On the other hand, if her constitution required her to sweat in another season, the same worker, to make it happen, would have to take suitable and expensive drinks.

As a conclusion to some practical experiments in beekeeping, Georges de Layens wrote: 'There is a benefit, all things being otherwise equal, to let the bees do their own construction'.

And in support of this statement, he cited the following paragraph from Abbé Deléphine:

'Given two hives of the same strength and two brood boxes of the same capacity, one fitted with embossed sheets and the other with empty comb from the extractor, which will be filled first? A priori, it seems that the second would be in advance of the first, the bees, in fact, having only to fill the cells with honey and seal them up. The experiments I have done with very great care have, however, given the opposite result'.

As for the straightness of comb, it is rarely obtained with wax foundation. The sheet of wax foundation, when it is in the hive, is subject to non-uniform temperatures: warmer at the top and cooler at the bottom, and that before it has been drawn, i.e. strengthened by the bees. On the other hand, comb built by the bees is only extended according to their needs, and it is totally covered with bees so all of it is at the same temperature. Moreover, the bees do not extend the comb without finishing it, without giving it its normal thickness. Comb is thus sturdier and better able to withstand variations in temperature if need be. Wax foundation, it is true, puts order in the hive and obliges the bees to build in the direction of the frames. But we get the same result, and more economically, with a simple starter of half a centimetre made of raw wax.

Wax foundation is no more able to find its *raison d'être* in the suppression of drones.

The queen (one in each hive) is mated only once in the four to five years of her life. Nature could not have provided thousands of drones each year just for mating. Therefore drones have another role in the hive.

In my childhood, I never heard males or drones mentioned. My father, like our neighbours, called them *couveaux* ('brooders'). I think that the basic role of drones is to keep the brood warm while the bees go to the fields. I see the proof of this in the following facts.

Bees do not get rid of the drones when their virgin queen has been mated. They do it only when the nectar flow has finished, i.e. when they no longer need to forage.

The drones only leave the hive other than for mating with the queen when the air temperature is very warm and during the hottest period of the day, i.e. when the brood does not need warming.

I have always noticed that the most productive hives have lots of drones.

I am therefore not of the opinion that we should try to reduce the number of drones.

In any case, wax foundation does not suppress them. The bees find a way of providing the queen with the number of drone cells she needs. They build them in the corners of frames. If need be they enlarge worker cells to make drone cells. And they do this right in the middle of a sheet of foundation. Moreover, the queen sometimes lays worker eggs in drone cells.

Simplifying the spring visit

Beekeeping textbooks recommend opening hives at a spring visit for four reasons:
- to see if the queen is present
- to check the state of the stores
- to clean the frames
- to start the renewal of comb.

The presence of the queen can be established without opening the hive. There is definitely a queen in the hive if the bees are bringing in pollen, if their coming and going is normal and steady, and if they do not show any concern, i.e. they do not appear to be looking for some lost treasure – their queen.

The stores will certainly be sufficient if they were made up in autumn as recommended.

But in modern hives you cannot do without the process of cleaning frames. For this, the frames have to be taken out one by one, the wood scraped on all surfaces to remove propolis. If this is not done every year, it becomes impossible to remove them without damaging them and without crushing lots of bees.

The combs have to be renewed every three years, four at most. Otherwise the cocoons that the bees leave in the cells when they hatch reduce cell volume. The bees that later hatch from those cells cannot develop fully. They are atrophied bees unable to do a great deal of work and, quite the opposite, very prone to contract any disease threatening their colony.

In the various manipulations during the season one has not always been able to move old frames to the sides of the brood box. The presence of honey or brood prevents this, for the brood must always be kept together and the honey should always be above or beside the brood. It thus often happens that in spring the old frames have to be replaced without being able to move them to one side. This is an additional complication to the spring visit.

In this operation there is a risk of crushing the queen between the frame uprights and the walls of the hive. Or equally, when the frame bearing the queen is replaced in the hive, glad at finding their queen after her short absence, the bees press themselves round her, surrounding her completely, squeezing and often suffocating her. Three quarters of queenless colonies are the result of manipulations in the hive.

In any case, cleaning the frames and removing the old ones should be done in spring, in our area in April, because at this time one is less hampered by brood, which is still not very advanced.

But in April, the temperature is not very high. Moreover, it is obvious that the work at this spring visit takes a certain amount of time. Also, I do not hesitate to point out that one man will not find sufficient sunny days in April each year between 11 a.m. and 2 p.m. to do the work this visit entails on fifty hives.

We designed our People's Hive to avoid opening the hive in spring by having hive-body boxes on top of each other and by enlarging the hive underneath and harvesting from the top. All the boxes come into our hands, one after the other, every three or four years. We profit from this by cleaning them and replacing comb in our workshop in winter when we have the time for it.

In spring, we need only clean the floor without opening the hive, without our having to be concerned with the outside temperature and without fear of crushing the queen. This work can be done at any temperature and at any hour of the day.

Simplifying enlarging the hive

Whereas the bees thrive better in a small hive in winter and spring, in summer they need lots of space. On the one hand, there is very significant chilling of the hive and stoppage of laying brood if enlargement is done early. On the other hand, if enlargement is done late, the bees have already prepared for swarming and nothing will stop them doing so. The swarm might then be lost. In any case, the honey harvest will be reduced. Good beekeeping guides have given wise counsel: put on the first super when all the frames in the brood chamber except the two at the extremities, one each side, are covered with bees, then put on the next super when the first is partly filled with honey.

However, this advice avoids neither cooling the brood chamber each time a super is added, nor a lot of work for the beekeeper. One may have to open the hive several times to check how many frames are occupied, for all the hives in a single apiary are not at the same stage. The same vigilance has to be exercised for the first supers. Here are the causes of repeated chilling of the brood chamber, which annoys and overtaxes the bees and increases work for the beekeeper.

Abbé Voirnot and de Layens had wanted to rectify these faults.

Abbé Voirnot adopted shallower supers, only 100 mm deep. The hive is not cooled as much when such supers are added. But then the beekeeper only has more inspections in order to decide when more supers should be added.

De Layens got rid of supers and increased the frames in the brood nest to at least eighteen instead of nine. In theory the bees will occupy all the frames according to their needs.

In the de Layens hive the part occupied by the brood does not lose heat suddenly but only loses some of it steadily. The problem is only lessened.

On the other hand, the beekeeper's work is increased. The bees put their honey over the brood chamber and some of it to the sides. As there are no supers on the de Layens hive the bees put their honey at the sides. Now the bees will not cross the honey to find a place for new brood or honey. They

141

prefer to swarm. In the de Layens hive, the bees are stuck between two frames of honey and therefore swarm, as if they were short of space, with several empty frames beyond those filled with honey. The beekeeper can certainly remedy this fault. If he moves the frames covered with honey away from the brood and replaces the frames containing honey with empty frames, the bees will not swarm, at least not from lack of room, but in these conditions the problem is worsened, and it is better if boxes are added vertically to the hive, both for the beekeeper and for the bees.

With the People's Hive, as we can increase its size from below, we can do this very early, and only once, with as many boxes as the strength of the colony demands. We avoid swarming through lack of space. We need not fear chilling the brood nor annoying the bees and we avoid a lot of trouble. When we have carried out this enlargement in April, in the Easter holidays if this time suits us, we leave the bees to their work and in peace and we need do no more than return to harvest the honey in August, during the summer holidays.

Furthermore, this enlargement of the hive from below is real and leaves the space freely at the disposal of the bees. In the People's Hive, as in all hives, the bees first deposit nectar near the entrance to save time, but in early evening they carry it to its final position above or beside the brood. The main cause of swarming, lack of space, is thus really reduced by our method.

One might argue that because with this method the honey would be harvested from combs that had contained brood and would thus always contain pollen, its quality would be poorer. But in the People's Hive, most of the pollen disappears with the brood. Only a little remains as is found in all hives, even in supers where there has been no brood.

As for combs that have contained brood, they only change the taste or the colour of the honey when they are black and spongy, because a fermentation has developed. But if our method is carefully followed such comb never occurs. Its place it taken by comb that is light-brown [*blond foncé*: – nearly the colour of hazelnut, *Tr.*] and with greater ease.

In other hives, the honey is first deposited in the bottom frames, and thus in frames that have contained brood. And it is not unusual for these frames to be black, therefore capable of changing the colour and taste of the honey, for, in these hives, the replacement of old frames is difficult and it is not uncommon that the beekeeper does not do it.

One may also argue that in the People's Hive, the honeys from different seasons are mixed.

But we have pointed out in another section that only mixed honeys are healthy and worth recommending. Moreover, in reality, the different honeys are only mixed at extraction. In the hive they are deposited one above the other in layers going from top to bottom, proportional in size to the forage at different times of the year.

If the beekeeper is interested in meeting the tastes of his customers, there is nothing to stop him from extracting a box or even a few combs from time to time.

Furthermore, it should be noted that the honey late in the season, generally the darkest, is placed at the bottom of the stores, and as a result immediately above the bee cluster. This will be the honey that the bees consume first and which should be left for them when preparing the hives for winter.

Simplifying the harvest

In our hive, as with others, the hive has to be opened and the bees have to be cleared with smoke. An entire super or hive-body box can be removed, or just individual combs.

It is only in adjusting the winter stores that there is a difference between our method and the others, but to our advantage.

In other hives, it is absolutely necessary to lift the frames in the brood chamber, whether the hive has too much honey or whether it does not have enough.

If there is too much honey, the development of brood in spring will be stopped – lack of space – and the wintering will be less successful. The bees always position themselves under the honey. The more honey there is above their cluster the more they must warm some empty and unusable space.

If there is not enough honey they have to be given some, preferably in frames, because in such hives feeding is more difficult and less rational than in the People's Hive. Results: time wasting, cooling the brood chamber, upsetting the bees. With our method there is no need to remove surplus stores because the surplus is minimal. In a People's Hive with fixed comb there are 48 square decimetres of comb. It should be left with 36 square decimetres of comb filled with honey. The difference, i.e. 12 square decimetres of comb, if ever there is brood, will be reduced to 3 or 6 decimetres at most, i.e. 1 to 2 kg of honey. This surplus can be left without any great difficulty.

If, on the other hand, the stores are insufficient, one can still avoid touching the comb in the brood chamber. This is the advice we give. All that is needed is to put under the brood chamber without opening it a hive-body box containing the feeder. The work is simplified. Our readers will understand after these reflections why we attach great importance to the size of the hive-body box. To respect the instincts of the bees we have to increase its volume and depth, but to avoid trouble and work for the beekeeper we have to keep it within limits. It is only after long trial and error that we have found the happy medium.

Simplifying transferring bees to another hive

Our method of driving bees differs in principle from others on one point: destruction of the brood.

For the brood is of no use during the nectar flow because it will arrive too late. The bees, moreover, will have time after the nectar flow to raise a new brood. Put another way, they will start raising it the same day that the old brood is destroyed.

The brood is even a disadvantage during the nectar flow because it keeps thousands of bees in the hive who could go out foraging. This is why leading beekeepers have tried to stop or reduce brood development during the nectar flow, even in established colonies.

The main thing when establishing a colony is to assure it food and shelter. It is therefore sensible to remove the obstacles that could prevent achieving this aim. And the brood is an obstacle, the main one.

This brood is absolutely essential, but, for a time, of secondary importance; and the bees, we can be certain, will not forget to raise brood either during the nectar flow or afterwards and all the less according to how rich they are in honey and drawn comb.

Simplifying artificial swarming

My method of artificial swarming differs from others on two points. It avoids for the beekeeper the problems of finding the queen and moving the combs. This work is always difficult and dangerous. Difficult, because, for any beekeeper, the queen is always like a needle in a haystack. Dangerous because in manipulating the combs one might squash the queen. In any case, the bees often get squashed and this annoys the whole colony.

Here, as always, I have as a goal the saving in time, warmth and honey and respect for the irritability of bees. We have seen that the beginner can do this work as well and as quickly as an experienced beekeeper. There is no need to be good at recognising a queen.

Simplifying finding the queen

I do not advise looking for the queen, not even for renewing the blood of the apiary, because there is a ready opportunity to introduce a queen from elsewhere when artificial swarming is carried out.

But it may happen that there are years when no artificial swarming is done. We have given a simple, quick and certain method of finding the queen.

It is clear that this procedure can only be carried out with hives with boxes as in the People's Hive.

Larger cells

We have already said that the bees leave behind a cocoon in the cell from which they have hatched, which, by repetition, reduces the volume of the cell. The bees that hatch there are necessarily smaller, atrophied, less fitted for work, altogether disposed to suffer the illnesses and epidemics of their species.

But the method used in the management of the People's Hive allows frequent and easy renewal of all the comb, at least every three years. Therefore, with this method there are no small cells.

The volume and weight of the bees also has another significance. It allows them to gather pollen and nectar from more flowers. The snapdragon or antirrhinum, for example, is closed to many insects. Bumble-bees, because of their weight, manage to open this flower as they land on the lower lip. Honey bees also manage it when their baskets are sufficiently loaded with pollen. Their own weight therefore has an influence in this circumstance.

Less opening the hive

Each time we open a hive, even on the hottest days, we cool its interior. And this cooling is all the greater the longer we have the hive open and the cooler the air temperature. And this cooling, which upsets the bees and tends to make them angrier, obliges them to re-warm the inside of the hive as quickly as possible. The result is obvious: a loss of honey for the beekeeper and an over exertion not planned for by nature, a wasteful exhaustion, of the bee.

I am convinced that these hive interior inspections also weaken the bees, lead to their degeneration and make them more liable to contract all the diseases, that are not new, but are more frequent since the fashion for framed hives and the methods that go with them.

And it is clear that our method avoids lots of visits to the inside of the hive.

Frame beekeeping is difficult

Abbé Colin wrote: 'Managing a framed hive, on the evidence of its proponents, requires a superior intelligence, a thorough knowledge of the bee, great manual dexterity, and, I would add, lots of patience. All beekeepers have superior intelligence, perfect agreement on this point, but have they all the patience of an ox and the tread of a cat?'

Berclepsch [*sic*, probably Berlepsch, *Tr.*] goes as far as saying that among fifty beekeepers, there is hardly one combining the qualities needed to manage framed hives.

I am entirely of the opinion of M. Hamel when he says: 'With almost all the producers of honey who supply consumer demand, who perform economical and logical beekeeping, who produce at the lowest cost, we are of the school of fixed-comb beekeeping; with the amateurs, to inform oneself, to entertain oneself, to amuse oneself, we are with the school of frame beekeeping'.

Moveable frames do not exist in beekeeping

The frames in framed hives are only really moveable at their exit from the wood workshop.

For in a short time they develop adhesions between frames and between frames and hive walls. The bees deposit propolis which gradually gets thicker.

I do not hesitate to stress that the hives with frames are further from mobility of comb than hives with fixed comb. In any case, it is far easier to remove adhesions in a hive with fixed comb than in a framed hive. The wax comb does not resist the blade of a knife. Propolis offers more resistance and the knife often cannot even get between two pieces of wood.

It has been argued that in the People's Hive with fixed comb, adhesions may form between the combs of the tiered boxes, the bees having a tendency to extend the comb on top to the one below it.

In the Palteau hive, which we shall discuss, these adhesions are likewise produced. In this case, a steel wire has to be pulled through to cut the adhesions when a box has to be removed. Obviously, this procedure could cause the queen to be crushed (highly inconvenient), the death of several bees (whence irritation of the rest), leakage of the honey, therefore robbing.

But we do not have this problem in the People's Hive with fixed comb. If, as we recommend, the top-bars are properly positioned in the same vertical plane, if the hive is level, the bees cannot join the combs of the box above to that of the one below. To construct a comb, the bees are upside down under the combs. When they reach 4 mm above the top-bars of the box below they have to stop. Four millimetres is in fact the width of their bodies.

Granted the bees would be able to deposit propolis on the combs and fill in the gap separating the comb above.

In this case there would never be an adhesion between propolis and comb wax as strong as that between propolis and wood as occurs between frames and the walls of the hive.

Furthermore, in the People's Hive, the bees never have time to fill this gap because each box is harvested, emptied and cleaned every two or three years.

Moreover, as we recommend, each time a box is opened, the hive tool is passed over the top-bars and the top rim of the walls. The top of the top-bars is thus never long coated with propolis, not long enough for it to become thick enough to reach the comb above.

It is true that we recommend cleaning sufficiently to enable placement of the boxes by sliding horizontally. For sliding them is far better than putting them on vertically.

The failure of modern beekeeping

Framed hives have been available to beekeepers for fifty years. An open book, they say, at least a book that one can open at will. No more mysteries in the life of the bee; no obstacles to help her and guide her in her work. Therefore very considerable advantages for the practice of beekeeping.

And lots of companies have been started to supply these hives together with their multitude of accessories. And each year beekeepers are offered new models said to be more productive, novelties created by skilful woodworkers. I know them well.

And many magazines are published whose articles allow the reader to differentiate the truth from the lies.

But I have been able to notice from fifty years of practising beekeeping in big apiaries and from observations amongst my numerous contacts, that no modern beekeeping method has been able to be sustained without diseases increasingly developing in the apiaries, and that honey is difficult to sell (in normal times, of course).

No modern beekeeping enterprise has been sustainable

I still know of many apiaries of various sizes where the old skeps in various forms have been used for several generations. I know the profits of some of these apiaries. And these profits greatly exceed those of the best industries.

On the other hand, I can confirm that no modern beekeeping enterprise has been sustainable. Their owners have had to abandon the enterprise because it did not feed them. Or they have grafted on to the enterprise some kind of business, be it confectionery, mead, encaustication, polish, beekeeping equipment, etc. In which case the apiary becomes an advertisement... .

Only people who have time to spare and their living secured are able to sustain these modern hives, among them teachers, parsons, and all kinds of bureaucrats. It is because of this that beekeepers from self-interest have considered stopping all bureaucrats from practising beekeeping.

Diseases develop increasingly in modern apiaries

I would really like a hive to be a book but I am sure that it should remain almost always shut. Bees like solitude. Therefore opening the hive goes against the bees. It obliges them to make a continuous over exertion to re-warm the brood chamber. Modern methods, in other ways that I speak about in my book, also force the bees into harmful overwork. And overwork leads to weakening and weakening makes them more prone to contracting any disease. It is the same with bees as it is with people.

Queen breeding, artificially of course, is also a cause of failure. We discuss this too in our book.

And diseases develop increasingly in modern apiaries, above all foulbrood, the awful foulbrood.

People call in vain for visits by distinguished veterinarians, for remedies from knowledgeable chemists, for registrations and sacrifices from beekeepers. It is the cause that should be eliminated. Let us stop going against the instincts of bees. Let us stop ignoring her needs. Let us obtain healthy bees in skeps and, above all, let us not feed bees on sugar.

The writer, Caillas, condemned the People's Hive because it prevented in a way almost all application of modern methods which are the future of beekeeping.

But I do not hesitate to point out that modern methods will lead beekeeping to destruction and that only skeps and the People's Hive will save it.

Honey is difficult to sell

Honey is the only healthy sugar; that is obvious. But beet sugar is so easy to use that it is the preference of ignorant or lazy housekeepers. And it is so cheap that it is also preferred by the poor, young and old.

What should be done? Produce honey cheaply so it can be sold at the price of beet sugar with a reasonable profit. In these conditions honey would find its clientele again from amongst all the wise people in the world.

Can this aim be achieved? Yes, I believe it can. But on condition that beekeeping is carried out with less expensive hives and according to a method more economical on the beekeeper's time and more respectful of the needs of the bee.

The People's Hive is not a revolution in beekeeping

After the first editions of this book people said to me that the People's Hive is an innovation, a real revolution in beekeeping.

It is not. To design the People's Hive I was inspired by skeps where bees have lived for centuries. I was also inspired by the most natural hive, certainly the oldest, namely the hollow tree. To design the People's Hive I had also studied the Dadant hive and its opponents: the Sagot hive, the Voirnot hive, the de Layens hive.

Furthermore, when I published a monthly journal, some subscribers told me about the pyramidal hive and the Palteau hive.

The Pyramidal Hive

Here are some extracts from a book in the National Library: *The Pyramidal Hive, simple and natural method for constantly raising all bee colonies and for obtaining from each colony each autumn the harvest of a full basket of wax and honey, without contaminants, without brood, furthermore several swarms* (C. Decouédic, President of the Canton of Maure, Département d'Ille-et-Vilaine, 2nd ed.; Mrs. Vve. Courrier, ed., publisher, Librairie pour la Science, Quai des Augustins, No. 57, Paris, 1813).

1st On the design of the pyramidal hive.

'In the wild state bees work from top to bottom, never from bottom to top, as long as there is still space inside.

'In working downwards, they leave their earlier constructions above their later work, to continue work only on the latter, in which the queen mother, likewise having descended, lays her new brood under the protection of the whole colony. In the second year there is no brood or bees in the upper layers of comb. They are totally full of honey.

'That is the way the bee works in the wild state. It is not difficult to apply this art of arrangement to the execution and use of three boxes placed at the return of each spring, one under the other, to form the pyramidal hive, whose top hive body, free of bees and brood but full of honey, is each year without interruption always at the disposal of the owner. It is sufficient each spring to put one hive below the other because the bees go down there when the top one is full. At the second spring there are three boxes underneath each other and at the following autumn one removes the top hive-body or box. And thereafter in perpetuity in spring there is one box to be put underneath the two left for the autumn and winter, and one hive-body or box to remove each autumn.

'The Pyramidal Hive is 9, 10 or 11 *pouces* in diameter and height, 27, 30 or 33 *pouces* for the three hive-body boxes, i.e. a maximum of 297 mm diameter and 891 mm deep, and 20.5 litres for each box.' (see footnote p. 148)

The Palteau Hive

Another work was published at Metz, by Joseph Colignon, in 1756, under the title *Novel construction of hives in wood, including the method of managing the bees, invented by M. Palteau, First Clerk of the Bureau of General Supplies of Metz.*

Here are the main points by which these hives approach the People's Hive:

One hive is made of several boxes, all the same size, interchangeable and square. The author writes on page 35: 'I can also adjust the size of my hives to all the swarms that are presented; one box or two, more or less goes to make up the hive I have chosen, a very suitable home for the colony that has to live in it'. He writes: 'That also avoids having all sorts of hives of different sizes to receive different swarms'. A hive is: 'a box which is one *pied* square by three *pouces* deep, including the bottom, which should be three *lignes* thick[1]. In the middle of the bottom (which in reality is the top) there is an opening seven and a half inches square. The rest of the bottom is pierced with small holes. The holes are to save the bees time in making wasteful detours when passing from one box to another.'

The bees attach the combs to this ceiling, as they do to bars which appear to have been introduced by Della Rocca. The square opening in the ceiling allows the bees to continue the middle comb without stopping while preventing a gap, and to facilitate the movement of the queen from one box to another. To cut the joined comb the author uses a steel wire which he passes between the boxes like a cheese-wire. Each box has 'its own entrance for the bees. When several boxes are combined only the entrance of the bottom box is left open'. These days, there is no longer any need to be concerned with this important detail, thanks to the system with the entrance in the floor.

The whole is placed on a fixed board forming the floor, then covered with an 'overcoat' which makes it double-wall.

The method of managing the bees differs in that enlargement and feeding is from the bottom which avoids chilling. Harvesting is from the top. The author smokes the bees to make them go down into the lower boxes. On page 32 he writes: 'I oblige them to go down into the lower boxes and to leave me at liberty to work in peace. Moreover, I am assured of getting the best honey which is always at the top of the hive and to leave them only the mediocre which suffices for them to go through winter. No more am I concerned about touching the brood and detaching it because it is situated only in the middle and at the bottom of the hive'.

Here, dear readers, are practical, logical hives. They are not perfect, but their faults are minimal. Eminent beekeepers such as de Layens, Abbé Voirnot and Abbé Sagot, would have made light of eliminating them. If these masters had only had to perfect our old French hives, instead of fighting the Dadant Hive, it is likely that I would have found the People's Hive as it is in its present form.

I would have saved twenty years of research, work and expense. For, if, in fact the People's Hive came out of those of Layens and Voirnot, it is no less true that the People's Hive has the same principles as the Decouédic and Palteau hives.

De Layens thought that our modern beekeeping methods demand too much time and expense of the beekeeper. Abbé Voirnot and Abbé Sagot considered them contrary to the needs and instincts of bees. Our own studies have led us to the same conclusions.

De Layens, Abbé Voirnot and Abbé Sagot must have known of the hives of Decouédic and Palteau. These hives must not have been forgotten in their time like mine. They did not believe they should be concerned with them.

---

[1] *pied (du roi)* = foot = 324.83 mm; *pouce* = inch = 27.069 mm; *ligne* = line = 2.256 mm *Tr.*

Fascinated by the undeniable advantages of the extractor, and believing that frames are necessary in order to use it, they only bothered with framed hives. They did not have time to recognise their mistake and to start new trials.

Having come after them, I have profited from their successes and their failures. It is thus by a different route that I have pursued the same goal. I believe I have reached it.

De Layens, Abbé Voirnot and Abbé Sagot have no less right to the recognition of all beekeepers, especially mine. It is their work I continue in publishing this book.

Will I be heard? Certainly not.

Anatole France wrote: 'If you try to instruct your teacher, all you do is humiliate and anger him'. Anatole France was right to generalise. There are people who are more intelligent than proud. I address myself to those.

In any case, I have the satisfaction of being able to say at the end of my days that I have worked for the return to the land. For I am a son of the soil and a disciple of the great Sully.

Poets have said: 'To live to a great age is to outlive one friends. To live to a great age is to outlive the trees one has planted. To live to a great age is to outlive illusions. Yes, more's the pity! But to live to a great age is also to enjoy one's experience. To live to a great age is also often to achieve a goal pursued for a long time. To live to a great age is also sometimes to succeed in being useful for longer. Sweet old age!'

Intensive beekeeping

In beekeeping, as in many other areas of production, it is the scramble for millions. I regret to say to my readers that this scramble for millions is a scramble to the death.

I was young once. I believed I could practice artificial breeding of queens successfully. But I realised that apart from one good queen, I provided only mediocre and inferior queens. I gave up this breeding because I wanted to be honest.

I practised a method where colonies worked together (*Capucine d'Angers*). Great expense, lots of work, numerous queenless colonies, problematical results, in any case always insufficient. I abandoned this method which, moreover, has not been mentioned for a long time.

And intensive modern methods do not attract me: stimulatory feeding, queen excluders, heating the hive, two-queen systems, superposition of colonies, etc. I only try them for what catches the eye of any beekeeper who is a little experimental.

Over exertion weakens the breed

I have certainly seen the research on over production in poultry farming, for example. Specimens with high productivity have been obtained. But on the other side there are infirmities, illnesses, mortalities previously unknown. From this fact, overall production is on the whole reduced and the breed is destroyed. As I see it, we are on our way towards doing the same thing in beekeeping. Already the steady progress of foulbrood is noticeable. The weakened stock no longer has the strength to destroy the microbes that it encounters.

I have known poultry farms where intensive egg production is practised. Production seems wonderful from November to February. In March, laying ceases and all the hens die if they are not sold for the table. To repopulate the hen house they have to go to other breeders.

This is why I am convinced that intensive modern beekeeping methods will lead to the success of skeps and the People's Hive, which alone conserve the stock.

The variations in temperature frequently cool the hives down and forces the bees to over exert themselves to re-establish the normal temperature. Frequent opening of the hives increases their over exertion even more.

Finally, artificial breeding that is practised in intensive beekeeping only gives mediocre and inferior queens. Again, the stock will not benefit from this.

As a result people will end up only with bees that are weak, poor workers, incapable of resisting disease, above all foulbrood.

Intensive methods bring risky profits

The aim of these methods is to obtain big populations at the beginning of the nectar flow. This is clearly the way to get big harvests.

But the date of the nectar flow cannot be forecast a month in advance. The temperature may advance or delay it by eight days, which adds up to a variation of fifteen days. Therefore sometimes beekeepers are ready too soon, sometimes too late; whence a waste effort if they are ready too late, and onerous work if too soon, for it is necessary to feed the weak colonies generously.

Practising intensive methods is dangerous

Doubling colonies (one on top of the other) is even more dangerous than other intensive methods.

In spring there are often big drops in temperature. The colonies at the bottom always suffer most from such drops in temperature, resulting in brood death and all its consequences.

Practising intensive methods is very expensive

To use these methods specially-made very expensive hives are required. In any case, it is necessary to use a certain number of specially-made, thus also very expensive, excluders. This results in a bigger capital expenditure which reduces the real profit from the method.

Furthermore, to handle whole hives of this kind you need to be a market porter or have strong helpers who are used to bees. It should not be forgotten that propolis, the stickiest of adhesives, always complicates the work. This results in a new source of expense.

Practising intensive methods takes a lot of time

All these methods call for a lot of work. Putting colonies one above the other even requires such demanding work that the beekeeper will not be able to apply himself to any other job. This is not the case with most beekeepers. For them, beekeeping is a supplementary job.

It should be noted that the practice of intensive methods irritates the bees and sometimes makes them unmanageable whatever their breed, because frequent opening of the hive and cooling of the brood necessarily upsets them.

Without fearing contradiction, I state that the work demanded by a group of four hives managed intensively would allow the management of an entire apiary of People's Hives. For such an apiary will yield more honey with less worry, especially if our pioneering method is used, a method without risk and which does not overwork the bees. It eliminates temporarily pointless work (raising brood) for them and allows them to get on with fruitful work (harvesting honey).

Pastoral beekeeping

Pastoral beekeeping is an important method of increasing production. By practising it, bees are given the opportunity for making successive moves to different plants: oilseed rape, early sainfoin, lime trees, acacia, late sainfoin, buckwheat, heather, etc., etc... .

The only problem is the transport of hives at the time when these plants are in flower. But the People's Hive is well suited to doing this. The hives are placed on a trailer in two rows with the entrances outwards. A passageway can be arranged between the rows, in which case the trailer will need to be 1.6 metres wide.

I think it is preferable to give the hives all the boxes they may need before leaving. In this case, the passageway is unnecessary and the trailer need be only one metre wide.

Furthermore, the length of the trailer will be that which leaves a maximum space of 600 mm for each hive. It is helpful to make a few holes in the bottom of the trailer for water to flow out.

The hive floors are fixed to the floor of the trailer with two nails or two screws. The hive is placed on the floor. But it is important that the floors and the boxes are fixed together with lockslides.

Whatever time of day the move is made, use our perforated entrance and our mesh hive cover. At the destination, use our flat roof which sheds water to one side and to the outside of the trailer. At the end of all the nectar flows, the trailer is brought back to the workshop for extracting the honey.

Hefting the hive

We have described how a check can be made on hive stores by counting the number of square decimetres of honeycomb. Some beekeepers have found this method difficult. We have designed a hefting tripod for them. It comprises a tripod and a plate supporting the hive, a spring balance and a lever.

Method of use

Remove the hive roof and quilt.

We have a hive that has been given two boxes of drawn comb, one of which is brood and the other honey.

It is a question of how much of it contains honey. Place the tripod in front of the hive 5 cm away with the un-raised foot under the hive. Put the plate under the hive, keeping behind the hive; insert under the hive the two small arms of the plate and push them up to the front feet of the hive; lift the three steel wires fixed to the arms of the plate; attach these to a spring-balance; attach the spring-balance to the lever, fix the lever on the tripod; depress the lever. The balance will indicate the gross weight of the hive.

From the gross weight subtract 8 kg for two boxes of drawn comb, 2 kg for bees and brood, 1.5 kg for the hive floor, 1.75 kg for four cast-iron legs or 0.75 kg for four wooden legs as required, the weight of the metal plate of the tripod.

If the hive has no legs, put the plate next to the hive. Put the hive without its floor on this plate and proceed as before. Knowing the weight of honey contained in the hive it is only necessary to make this weight up to 12 kg. This is easily done in one night with our large feeder, or two nights at most.

Conclusion

The People's Hive is a logical hive

Economical in design, economical in method, the People's Hive is a really logical hive.

In winter, there is no risk of the bees getting cold, provided that the stores are above the cluster of bees.

In winter, the bees cluster under the honey in an elongated shape (like a large pear with the stalk at the bottom). In the cluster there is a continuous movement of alternation. The bees at the centre rise towards the stores and eat a small quantity of honey. Warmed by this consumption of honey they descend via the periphery and warm their sisters. The latter rise in their turn to the stores and it continues like this throughout the winter.

It is thus important that the hive is tall enough to allow the stores to be placed above the cluster of bees, but not so large that the cluster of bees has to move sideways to find the stores. For, at the side of the bee cluster there will not be the same temperature as above.

This therefore counts against long shallow frames and shows the obvious superiority of the People's Hive whose two combs on top of each other give a width of 300 mm and a depth of 420 mm.

In winter, the bees abhor damp. But there is always a lot of damp in a hive. It comes from outside and it is produced by the drying of nectar and the respiration of the bees.

In a wide hive, the damp air flows from the bee cluster, which is a source of heat, and then cools, condenses and settles on the exterior walls and the outer frames of the hive, turning them mouldy and this accumulates to the great detriment of the bees.

In a narrow hive like the People's Hive, this dampness cannot travel from the bee cluster, nor cool, nor condense. It remains above the cluster of bees and ends up by escaping through the cloth covering the top-bars of the upper box and then passes into the quilt. And this is under the control of the bees who regulate this escape of moisture by putting more or less propolis on the cloth.

This therefore argues against crown boards or oilcloths often used to cover hives, and against wide hives such as the Dadant. Here the superiority of the People's Hive is its narrowness and cloth covering.

In a good season, the bees have to maintain enough heat over the brood (eggs and larvae). And they can obviously maintain this heat more easily over a surface of 300 x 300 mm than over a surface of 450 x 450 mm.

Once again this shows the superiority of a narrow hive like the People's Hive.

However, in the warm season, the bees need a lot of space and this varies a lot. But we can give them this space generously and timely, because we increase the size of the hive from below as we wish, without danger of chilling.

The People's Hive does not turn stones into honey; it will not give you honey without some work. No. But the People's Hive saves you a lot of expense, a lot of time and several kilogrammes of honey each winter. In a word, the People's Hive is a practical and logical hive. It will bring happiness to you and your bees.

For, in using the People's Hive with fixed combs you will certainly provide the most pleasant and most logical home for your dear bees – 'these benevolent messengers scented with the germs of life, winged more than wind, more discerning and reliable, who ceaselessly improve immortal nature. These humble gatherers of a bounty that belongs to you, which they watch over with great care, that they defend at risk of sacrificing themselves in death, that they are far from squandering because they do not touch it at all, unless it is to add to it and to look after it'.

Therefore go, my People's Hive, go into all the gardens of France. Go and give the children some nourishing sandwiches, and give the grown ups wellbeing in body and mind. Go and remind everyone of the necessity of work, the gentleness of unity, the beauty of devotion, the prosperity of countless families. Go and fill every fireside with honey and happiness. *Mella fluunt tibi.*

SIMPLIFIED ECONOMIC PRODUCTIVE METHOD
NO FRAMES – NO WAX FOUNDATION – LITTLE WORK

Breaking trust

The People's Hive has been copied in many regions where it is sold under different names: People's Hive; Warré Hive, Warré-type Hive. Certain less scrupulous people have given it their own name, advertising it with the two main features of the People's Hive: no frames, no wax foundation.

I have seen several of these hives. In general they have not been carefully constructed. Several people have added whimsical modifications which are far from being improvements. Among them are some silly modifications which do not allow application of our method.

Appendix

Warré beekeeping e-group where it is possible to get support from Warré beekeepers worldwide: *http://uk.groups.yahoo.com/group/warrebeekeeping*

The Warré beekeeping English web portal links to Warré material in several languages including practical advice with illustrations: *http://warre.biobees.com/index.html*

Plans of the Warré hive: *http://selbstversorgerforum.de/bienen/bilder/Emile_Warre_Technische_Zeichnungen_engl.pdf*

CPSIA information can be obtained at www.ICGtesting.com
Printed in the USA
BVOW030423270213

314233BV00003B/58/P

9 781904 846529